50 things
you need to know

SUPER
BRIGHT
BABY

John Farndon

Quercus

Contents

With many thanks to Early Years Professional Olga Nakston for her invaluable advice and ideas.

Introduction

The arrival of a new baby in the world is, for parents, one of the most amazing experiences imaginable.

Even though you know that millions upon millions of people go through the same thing every year, it seems miraculous. And that's exactly how it should be. Your baby is your own very special gift and because of that you will know instinctively what is right for him or for her in a way that is far beyond any book to advise.

Yet it can be daunting. You want the very best for your children. You want them to grow happy and bright, and face the world with joy and the ability to make the most of their potential – and then you realize that it's all up to you. Suddenly the prospect of being the best possible parent can seem just a little bit unnerving, and that's where this book aims to help.

This book gathers together 50 of the most important ideas from scientific and childcare experts on child development. Covering the period from late pregnancy to two years of age, these ideas will give you a grounding in the relevant neuroscience and psychology that are important in helping your child to develop healthily, happily and perfectly able to meet life's challenges with confidence – whatever they are.

What's interesting is that all the experts agree that the most important thing – in terms of brain development and physical and emotional wellbeing – is that your baby is truly loved and cherished. This book shows you how and why this is true, and why it's so important to acknowledge that ultimately, you're the expert on your own child. Every baby is unique, and your job is to nourish that individuality to its fullest potential. This book will give you the skills and knowledge you need to help your child become a truly super-bright baby.

John Farndon

1 Nourishing baby

It's important to eat well during pregnancy, to ensure that your body can supply all the nutrients your baby needs to develop and maximize her growing brain's potential. By the time she is born, your baby's brain will have grown more than 100 billion neurons.

Steady meals

Before you start to worry too much about your eating habits, though, just relax. Becoming stressed about what you should or shouldn't eat can actually be more harmful to your developing baby than any amount of dietary deficiencies. So allow yourself to be flexible about what you eat and when.

In essence, all you really need is a normal balanced diet to give your baby's brain a good start in life in the womb. This means plenty of fresh fruit and vegetables every day, some calcium-rich dairy foods, a few helpings of lean meat, fish, chicken or legumes, and some carbohydrates, such as bread, rice or pasta. If you eat a reasonably healthy diet already, simply keep an eye on your fat intake, raise your carbohydrates slightly and eat a little more fruit and vegetables than usual.

Extra carbohydrates are necessary because your body needs extra energy to carry a baby. Just how much extra depends on your normal weight and fitness, but it's likely to be about 15–20 per cent – a boost from, say, 2,000 calories a day to 2,300. Bear in mind that although you're eating for two, the second person in the equation is only around the size of a pea during the first trimester. During the third trimester, as the baby approaches birth weight, you'll need to boost your intake to around 2,500 calories a day.

Your body needs up to a third more protein than usual to provide the growing baby with the nutrition necessary for brain development. If you're a vegetarian, think about increasing your intake of protein-rich foods such as legumes, soy, quinoa, couscous, nuts and seeds. Pregnant women also need additional iron (from things like beef, dried fruit and soy) to build red blood cells, especially in the later months. You'll need lots of calcium and vitamin D in your diet (from cheese and milk) to build your baby's teeth and bones, and plenty of water, because your blood volume goes up 50 per cent when you're pregnant.

Brain boosters

Some foods and nutrients are thought to be specifically important to brain development. Folic acid, also known as vitamin B9, sits at the top of this list. A baby's brain and nervous system starts developing in the first few months of pregnancy with the growth of a groove of neural cells; these curl round to form a tube that will become the brain and spinal cord. Folic acid plays a key role in developing the genetic material for neural cells, and if this is deficient in early pregnancy, the neural tube may not develop properly, and can this lead to brain and spinal cord abnormalities such as spina bifida. You can obtain folates naturally by eating green leafy vegetables, asparagus and fortified cereals, but as the level of folic acid is critical in the first six weeks of pregnancy, doctors recommend taking a multivitamin supplement that includes 0.4 mg of folic acid.

In recent years, a lot of people have talked about how oily, cold-water fish such as herrings are the ultimate brain food. Fish oil is rich in the fatty acid omega-3, which is thought to have a wide range of benefits. One form of omega-3 called DHA (docosahexaenoic acid) makes up a significant portion of the membranes of neurons, a type of nerve cell – the brain is made up of around 100 billion neurons. DHA also

Foods to avoid

On the whole, most foods that form part of a normal healthy diet are fine to eat when you're pregnant. But these are no-nos:

- Alcohol, except in really small amounts; alcohol can cross the placenta. A recent study suggests that even moderate amounts of alcohol in pregnancy can lower a child's IQ.
- Rare meat and raw egg mayonnaise, which can be a source of toxoplasmosis. This produces flulike symptoms in mum but can be devastating for baby.
- Fish containing concentrations of mercury from pollution such as mackerel, shark and swordfish.
- Liquorice. Surprisingly, a study in Finland, where young women eat a lot of liquorice, showed that children of mothers who ate a lot of liquorice when they were pregnant did less well in cognitive tests at 8 years old and showed poor attention.

encourages the production of BDNF (brain-derived neurotrophic factor), which helps promote new neuron growth and connections. One scientific study suggested that when women ate more oily fish during the second trimester, their babies did better on mental development tests at six months of age. However, don't overdo it: two portions of oily fish a week (about 140 g/5–6 oz each) is probably enough. Also, avoid fish which are likely to have high levels of mercury (see box, opposite).

> Found great recipe for salmon stuffed with spinach and cream cheese. Delicious! And good for baby! #yummymummy

Other essential nutrients

Other significant nutrients for brain development include choline, iodine and copper. Choline (found in milk and eggs) helps form cell membranes and is important for the formation of blood vessels, including those now forming in your baby's brain. Dairy products, eggs and seafood are rich in iodine, which is necessary for healthy brain and nervous system development. Mushrooms and tinned tomato purée are very rich in copper, which is important for the formation of neurotransmitters (the chemicals that carry signals in the nervous system).

If you aim to 'eat the rainbow' – eating vegetables of every colour – and have a good protein and carbohydrate intake, you'll receive all the nutrients you need for a happy, healthy baby.

Condensed idea
Eliminating stress and focusing on relaxation will give your baby the best start

2 Prepped and ready

Pregnancy can be tiring and it can seem as if you have little time to spare. But if you can find a moment or two, it is well worth finding out not only what to expect when your baby arrives, but also what he will need from you to become a truly super-bright baby.

Mental preparation

There's all kinds of medical advice readily available to help you through the physical aspects of pregnancy and prepare for your baby's arrival. But what can you do to prepare the right mental environment?

The first thing is to understand the importance of your own wellbeing as parents. This is because it's essential for you and your baby to bond in a safe, stress-free environment – and that environment is essentially the space and love you provide. This means that it's not enough to think only about your baby – you need to think about yourself and your health and happiness. If you are happy and confident, your baby will be too. The curiosity and inquisitiveness that's so central to the bright baby depends on his

> Just been on a 'babymoon' in Spain to celebrate the first ultrasound. Now totally relaxed. #muminbliss

feeling secure in the world. If you're still struggling with emotional problems, you're likely to pass on strong negative feelings, such as fear or anxiety, without even realizing it. So as you're thinking about healthy eating and nursery preparations, take time, too, to think about

Watching other parents

Build your confidence as a prospective parent by finding out as much as you can about real parents and babies. Theories are great, but there's nothing like watching parenting in action to give you a genuine sense of what it's like to look after a child.

- Spend time around other babies. Research has shown that brain changes that encourage nurturing behaviour occur as a result of pregnancy and when people spend time looking after babies. You might not feel any different, but being around babies will actually change your brain to prepare for parenting.
- Do lots of research. Some of us are lucky enough to have been taught great parenting skills by our parents, but many prospective parents feel that they're lacking in the necessary skills and hands-on know-how. Check out some of the parenting website forums, where real parents offer support and solutions to each other.
- Visit baby classes, such as baby massage or swimming, that you might like to consider joining with your own child.

ways to feel happy and secure in yourself and about the pregnancy. Not everyone's circumstances are comfortable, of course, and many people's lives are beset by genuine problems over which they have no control; this is a good time to take stock of exactly what you can and can't control, changing what you can and accepting what you can't. As you wait for the big day when your baby arrives, set yourself the goal of making yourself as happy and relaxed as possible for the early days of his life. Consciously choose it, and think about how you might make it happen.

Fix any irritations

If there are practical irritations in your life, this is the time to fix them. If a dripping tap needs attention, for instance, do it now. Of course, it makes little practical difference whether you do it now or after the baby arrives, and you may even think that once the baby arrives and you're off work, at least for a while, that you'll have more time to deal with things like this. But it's a question of mental preparation. If you sort out the tap now, you will have dealt with a source of irritation – and given yourself a sense of achievement. Some women like to find little ways of feeling better every day of their pregnancy, and fixing practical irritations can score surprisingly highly on the feelgood factor.

The same thing goes for emotional irritations, such as lingering bad feelings of any sort with family, friends or neighbours. Do whatever you can to iron things out with the minimum fuss and maximum generosity. This sounds self-evident, but it's surprising how many parents carry grudges right through to the moment of birth – and even heighten them as the tension of expectation mounts. Think about the fact that you want the world to be a loving, safe place for your baby to enter – a place free from emotional turmoil and full of caring people. This might help you to put your own issues into perspective and give you the incentive to make that difficult phone call or visit.

Have fun!

Above all, try to make pregnancy a pleasure, rather than something you have to endure in order to have a baby. Go to yoga classes, if that's what makes you relaxed. If you love swimming or taking long walks, go with your instinct and do those instead. Any form of gentle exercise will make you feel healthier and give you a positive sense of your own wellbeing and strength. Make time for really relaxing too, by going out to concerts or a movie with your partner or friends, and simply spending cosy time at home. One great thing about pregnancy is that you can indulge any whim you wish (within reason!) and people are generally happy to help.

Learning stories

Your pregnancy homework is also about preparing your mental resources for the new arrival. In the following chapter (pages 12–15) we'll show you how to create great 'baby spaces', but for now, focus on preparing yourself for becoming a parent. Journalling is a good way to document your pregnancy – write down everything you feel and perhaps your wishes too. Think about your family stories and the stories you loved as a child – these will allow you to remember your own childhood and think about the things you want – and don't want – for your baby. Talk to your parents, other family members and friends about their feelings and experiences of being or having a child. Immerse yourself in the brave new world you're about to enter – especially its stories and its songs, which you'll soon be giving to your own precious child.

condensed idea
Focusing on relaxation will give your baby the best start

3 Baby space

You can help your baby to thrive by creating a special space for her within your home; perhaps her own room or a part of the garden. Fill it with things that will enrich her sensory environment and stimulate her curiosity and visual vocabulary.

Creating a baby garden

One of the best areas that you can create for your baby at home is a special garden or nature space. It's great to expose babies to the sensations of the natural world at a very early age – the sights, smells, sounds, textures and even the tastes. This allows them to enjoy a wonderful array of sensations when their brains are richest in potential, and so they grow up able to appreciate them fully. Just as babies lose the nerve connections that allow them to hear certain nuances of language if they are not exposed to them early in life (see page 98), so it is with the sensations of nature.

Research also shows that babies find the natural world very calming, and the rich array of sensations may gently strengthen neuronal networks (the essential links for memory, reasoning and emotional intelligence) within their developing brains.

Young babies are only interested in the world immediately around them, so you don't have to create anything big. If all you've got space for is a window-box, or even a big pot, that's fine. The crucial thing is that it will be their space to enjoy and experience nature, and where they will feel secure and you'll feel safe to let them play. It's easy to make a simple nature space. Find a large wooden box or garden pot and fill it with completely new, fresh compost. Cover this with new play sand (you can buy this from baby-equipment shops). Plant your box or pot with a variety of non-toxic plants without thorns or spiky leaves (see box below for plant ideas).

Make a space that you love

It's very tempting to go overboard when preparing the nursery or baby corner – especially for your first child. But there's no need. A baby can't tell and won't care how much money and effort you've put into making that five-star baby base. And there's actually little or no scientific evidence to suggest that filling a nursery to the brim with all kinds of brain-stimulating toys and paraphernalia will actually make your baby brighter, whatever the claims of brain-training games and toy

Plants for your baby garden

Many kinds of plants are safe and pretty for a baby to touch. A few are even good to eat. Choose soft-leaved herbs and flowers of various colours and avoid plants that are poisonous or irritating to the skin.

- **Good plants:** parsley, basil, strawberries, peas, pot marigolds, violets, pansies, nasturtiums. The leaves on parsley and basil are edible, as are the flowers of marigold, pansy and nasturtiums – and of course the fruits of strawberries when they are ripe.
- **Plants to avoid:** azalea, cherry, foxgloves, hyacinth, hydrangea, lantana, laurel, lily-of-the-valley, privet, rhododendron, rhubarb, snowdrop, wisteria, yew.

makers. There is even a possibility that too much stimulation will make it hard for your baby to settle and sleep calmly. The emphasis should be on simplicity, practicality and comfort. Once the nursery has all the basic necessities, think next about making the space suit you. Of all the stimulating patterns and interesting shapes you can provide your baby with, the best by a long, long way is your face – and if it's happy, she'll feel secure. Your face is what she looks for and needs to get to know, well before and above anything else. In fact, a newborn really needs little else beyond her parents' full love and close attention. So think first and foremost about setting up the space so that you are happy and relaxed spending time there yourself. Adorn the space with simple pictures and objects that make you smile, and that you can enjoy with her when she comes along. Remember that when you're not there, she will be asleep for most of the time, so the decor's not really important.

Babies love colour

In the past, some scientists promoted the idea that the nursery should be filled with geometric patterns and stripes in black and white. This was because they believed that newborns could not see colours, and preferred

looking at high-contrast edges, because their vision isn't very sharp. In fact, it's now known that even when they're born most babies can distinguish 20 shades of grey (that's shades of grey that differ by only five per cent). And by nine weeks, they can see differences 10 times more subtle. So by two months a baby would have no problem distinguishing a white fluffy rabbit on a white sheet. They can also see colours as early as two weeks of age.

It's impossible to be sure what colours babies would prefer for their nurseries – or, more importantly – whether it matters. Some scientific papers suggest babies 'prefer' blues and purples, but all they are really saying is that some babies' attention is held more by these particular colours. What matters most is whether you feel comfortable and happy in the room. If strong colours make you feel wonderfully energized and content, these are the colours you should go for. If plain pastel colours make you feel more relaxed, choose those. Imagine being a mum or dad, and consider what feels right.

> My baby garden is planted with safe plants – but I still watch over my baby like a hawk. #greenfingers

The secret to your nursery or baby corner is filling it with things that you will enjoy showing your baby. If cute, handpainted penguins dancing on the wall make you smile, go for it. Because when your baby is with you, you'll talk to her about the penguins and laugh, and your baby will be engaged and entranced. And that's a baby who already wants to learn more about the world.

Condensed idea
Use pregnancy as a time for creating the perfect baby space

4 The developing brain

Every part of a baby's development inside its mother's womb is astonishing, but nothing is more extraordinary than the development of his brain. At a very early stage of pregnancy he begins to learn things – about himself, his home in the womb and even the outside world.

Rapid growth

A baby's brain starts to develop almost from the moment that a sperm penetrates the egg, and it develops at a mind-boggling rate. In every second of early pregnancy, a baby's brain grows 4,000 new primitive brain cells – that's almost 15 million every hour. By the second month of pregnancy, the primitive structures of the baby's brain – that will tell his heart when to beat, his lungs when to breathe, his body to how to balance – are already beginning to develop.

The astonishing growth of brain cells reaches a peak in the fourth and fifth months, then slows down a little. But this proliferation doesn't just create numbers. As the months progress, complex structures appear in the brain, and as they develop, many new brain cells (neurons) migrate to particular places in the outer regions of the brain. However, no one knows how these cells know where to go. The journey is dangerous, and even though they are sometimes guided on their way by the brain's scaffolding of glia cells

> I drank a lot of apple juice in the last months of pregnancy and now my little one definitely prefers apple-flavoured cereal! #fruitlover

(special cells that provide physical and nutritional support for neurons), some never make it, and scientists are currently researching the implications of this. When the neurons finally reach their destination, they stretch out their connectors to neighbouring neurons. At this point, the foetus starts to show new forms of behaviour, including alternating between periods of activity and rest, and even yawning!

By the eighth month of pregnancy, a baby has 200 billion neurons – twice as many brain cells as an adult. However, neurons that don't make good connections are eliminated in a process called apoptosis; half of the original neurons are wiped out in the last stages of pregnancy and early infancy. Those that do live on become stronger than before, which is why this brain cell culling is sometimes called 'neural Darwinism' – only the fittest survive. The neurons that do survive go on to make connections with other cells. Some scientists sum up the process quite neatly like this: 'neurons that fire together, wire together'. Those that die have not been stimulated, and so are not needed. Apoptosis clears away this 'dead wood' to give more space to the neurons that are clearly needed.

School womb

These new brain cells aren't just lying dormant, ready to fire up when your baby is born. They're up and learning barely 10 weeks into the pregnancy, as the developing baby tries wiggling his rudimentary limbs to see what happens. By 23 weeks or so, he can hear things and may feel and even taste things, too, as he gets food from your bloodstream.

Babies can hear sounds while in the uterus, and those that are heard regularly may shape their growing brains. The basic soundtrack of the womb is, of course, the soft thump of the mother's heartbeat, the gentle rasp of her breathing and the low roar of her bloodstream. But

An environment for life

Since the 10th century, Korean mothers have been practicing Taegyo, the belief that the foetal environment affects a baby for her whole life. According to Taegyo:

- The mother must avoid all emotional turmoil during pregnancy.
- From the moment the baby begins to hear in the fifth or sixth month, the whole family must create an environment of calm, love and happiness.
- Reading stories with strong emotional content fosters bonding and the emotional development of the unborn baby.
- Playing music promotes calmness and helps develop the right side of the brain, bringing better hearing, clarity of thought and emotional stability.
- Yoga after the fifth month of pregnancy helps relax the mother.

an unborn baby can almost certainly hear muffled sounds from outside the mother's body, too, and that has tempted many to talk about the 'Mozart effect'. This is an idea that developed in the 1990s, when some experts claimed that classical music could 'organize' the baby's brain. However, there is scant real evidence that it actually works – and some experts think there is a danger that too much stimulation could distress the baby. If you like classical music, by all means play it, but don't feel obliged to listen to it if you'd rather be listening to Adele.

Early learning

Nonetheless, there is no doubt that babies do learn in the womb, and while there's no sign that you can boost your baby's IQ, there are things that may help you build a strong bond with your baby or help him to feel at ease and secure – the essential groundwork for a super-bright baby. Reading stories may not turn a baby into an embryonic Einstein, but it means he will recognize his parents' voices before he is born, so you might like to read aloud once in a while, knowing that your baby will be listening. In addition, there is some evidence that a particular piece of soft music heard while in the womb will later comfort a newborn when he starts to cry. The effect is, of course, as much on you as him – because the music makes you feel at ease (as it did when you were pregnant), it makes him feel at ease too.

Some experts recommend that mothers go out of their way to bond with the baby long before the birth, caressing their tummies and murmuring to the baby continually. This is great if it comes naturally, but only then; what matters most is the mother's ease and emotional balance.

Condensed idea
Your baby starts learning from the moment his brain cells begin to develop in early pregnancy

5 Love is all you need

Recent neuroscience has proved an ancient belief: the most important thing you can give your baby is love. There is powerful evidence that practical intelligence is highly dependent on emotional wellbeing. Bonding is crucial to healthy brain development.

Psychological food for the brain

Most parents instinctively love their babies and want to look after them. They are not acting out of a sense of societal or moral obligation. So perhaps it's not surprising that recent studies have shown that this instinctive love provides the soundest, most important guide of all to helping a baby develop into a bright child.

Love impels a parent to give a baby all the nurture she needs, and it causes the baby to seek nurture from the best places possible – her mum and dad. Just as sunlight is necessary for flowers to grow, love provides the essential psychological food a baby's brain needs to grow and develop physically in the best form possible, and it helps her develop a vital sense of security.

Some scientists and educators use the word 'bonding' when they mean love, but love is actually far more than bonding because, as the next chapter about 'attachment' shows, what is crucial about love is not just a strong connection, like superglue, but something more enduring, bigger and more outward-looking. By loving your baby and letting her develop the trust that you're always there for her, she grows up feeling positive about the world – confident in exploring it and in building new human relationships in the future. This is the best start for a super-bright baby, and the legacy of love will sustain your child throughout her life.

What is sleep training?

Sleep training is the idea that babies can be
trained to sleep through the night. It emerged
from the behaviourist idea that babies need
training to cope with the harsh realities of the world, but many
experts now think it is wrong-headed, as it is better to respond
quickly to a baby's needs rather than to instruct her. It's also
possible that the idea of getting babies to sleep through the night
has more to do with the parents' needs than those of the baby.

However, a baby's wellbeing also depends on the happiness of her
parents, which is difficult to achieve in a state of overtiredness. For
this reason, many people find it useful to help their baby gently find
a sleep routine. After six weeks, set up an appealing bedtime routine,
such as a warm bath and a story (mainly for the reassuring sound of
your voice) and finally a feed. Put her down for naps at similar times
during the day if she's happy – but don't force it.

Behaviourist techniques

Love is so hard to quantify and seems so 'unscientific' that for a long
time scientists totally underrated its importance. In the last century,
this lack of appreciation for love in a baby's life led to some of the
most heart-rending and cruel scientific experiments imaginable.
Well-meaning scientists became convinced by behavioural experiments
– such as those of Russian physiologist Ivan Pavlov, who trained dogs
to salivate at the sound of a bell – that what really mattered in child-
development was training. They reasoned that the best way to bring a
baby to its full development was to train its behaviour in just the same
way Pavlov's dogs were trained to salivate.

One of the originators of this behaviourist approach was American psychologist John Watson, who argued that too much love and affection left children ill-equipped to face the tough adult world. Consequently, many genuinely caring parents in the 1940s and 50s fought their natural instincts to love and cuddle their babies. Instead, they treated their babies with the minimum affection, following advice to avoid touching or holding them (as much as possible) and to put them to sleep alone, ignoring any crying.

Mum says I'm too soppy about my baby and that she needs to learn about life. Oops! Utterly wrong! #lovemybaby

The damage done to babies brought up in this way – and to their parents – doesn't bear thinking about, and no childcare expert today would encourage parents to act in this way. There are still plenty of experts who advocate 'sleep training' (see page 21) but their approach is now entirely different.

Always help a crying baby

Of course, the parents' instinct was right. A growing conviction that the hands-off approach must be wrong has been backed up by a wealth of scientific research that has confirmed how genuinely damaging a lack of love can be to the developing brain. The stress that results from an early feeling that no one loves you can actually stop the development of brain connections in the crucial early months when the baby's cortex (the outside of the brain responsible for 'higher' or more complex thinking) is growing very quickly.

If a baby is left to cry for a very long time, she may go quiet and stop crying, but that's because she is simply shutting down to concentrate on survival. While crying, she will experience an increase in heart rate, blood pressure and respiration as stress hormones course through her body. If she is exposed to these stress hormones for long, their effect

can be damaging. If the baby eventually decides that no one is coming to help her, she will retreat from the external world into her internal one, and the hormones released at this point can also harm her fragile, growing brain.

So what can you do in practical terms? The simple answer is to follow your instincts. Don't feel that you're somehow not 'toughening her up'. If your baby cries, respond to her as quickly as you can. Work on building an emotional bond right from the start and keep going. Don't just feed and clothe your baby and put her to sleep – respond to her with as much love as you can, staying alert to any sign of a smile or interest and giving it back generously. And of course cuddle, kiss and tickle her as much as you think she wants.

Condensed idea
The best possible 'technique' for ensuring your baby develops well is love

6 Getting attached

Over the last few decades, attachment theory has become one of the key theories of child development. It's now widely accepted that every baby needs to form a strong attachment to a primary caregiver. There are strategies you can use to strengthen this attachment.

The power of attachment

After World War II, it became clear to British psychiatrist John Bowlby that children – especially babies – who had been separated from their mothers during the war were not merely unhappy but actually suffered from arrested mental and physical development. From his research, and that of American-Canadian psychologist Mary Ainsworth, there grew a body of thought known as 'attachment theory', which completely overturned earlier ideas on child development. This is now the dominant scientific view. One idea it rejected, controversially at first, was the old belief in 'cupboard love' – the notion that babies love their parents simply because they provide food. Famous but rather sad experiments on baby rhesus monkeys separated from their mothers in the 1950s confirmed just how wrong this notion was, even for monkeys. The baby monkeys did not become 'attached' to a feeding nipple attached to a hard block, but instead chose to cling to a softer towelling block with a face, even though it offered no food.

> I used to let my moods dictate my baby's – but I've just realized that I need to pick up on hers! #Iseeyoubabe

Attachment and depression

Mothers who suffer postnatal depression or other stresses in the months after giving birth may find it hard to form an attachment with their baby. The effect on the baby can be long-lasting, and the lack of attachment can also increase the mother's sense of inadequacy and depression. Any woman finding it hard to form an attachment with their baby, or respond naturally to his or her needs, is likely to benefit from extra support. This may come from a doctor, family, online peer groups or friends.

Sometimes help with non-parenting tasks can make a big difference, such as asking others to assist with cleaning or cooking. Time away from the baby – such as having coffee with friends – can help a new mother make the transition from adult to parent more easily. Attachment is a two-way thing, and both mother and baby need to feel valued and supported.

Attachment theory is based on the idea that a warm, intimate relationship between an infant and parent is not just necessary for basic survival (the baby needs to 'bind' the parent to him to ensure the parent provides food and warmth) but it is also essential for ensuring full, healthy development throughout life. The baby's dependence on adults is not a problem to be overcome, as behaviourists thought (see pages 21–22), but must be seen as part of the whole growth process. It is no accident that as your baby develops some control over his movements, his first instinct is to reach towards mum or dad. Welcome this as a sign of healthy development; babies who have been deprived of attachment show reduced motor development and are unlikely to reach out.

Learning how to handle emotion

When your baby is born, he can feel deeply, and is driven this way
and that by his emotions. He cannot soothe himself by 'regulating'
his emotions. When he's distressed, he seeks the comfort of his carer
(normally his mum or dad) to help him. When you are always there to
respond to your baby in a sensitive way that shows you understand his
distress yet can offer comfort, he learns to trust that things will be all right
and that he has a safe place in the world – and he gradually learns from
you how to regulate his own emotions. The ability to 'self-soothe' like
this (moving from a feeling of distress back to calm) is vital for a baby to
learn, and will stand him in good stead as a child and an adult.

When your baby learns that you are always there to respond to his
emotional needs, he will feel able to explore his world, secure in the
trust that he will always find support and comfort when he needs it.
This is what is known as a secure attachment. Research confirms that

the regular physical contact, comfort and quick response to distress that underpin such secure attachments contribute hugely to intellectual progress. In practice, it means picking up and cuddling your baby when he is distressed, soothing him in the ways you've learned he really likes. As your baby grows from a child into an adult, you'll see his sense of secure attachment reflected in the way that he's able to form happy and satisfying relationships with friends, colleagues and those he loves.

Babies who are unable to form a secure attachment become emotionally unstable and preoccupied, and find it hard to communicate effectively with other people. But a baby who is able to form a secure attachment will feel safe, loved and confident – he will be more playful, less inhibited, very sociable and keen to start exploring his world.

Slow growing security

Attachments grow slowly and continuously, so for the first six months your baby needs to have one person who will always be there for him, looking after all his needs. Ideally, this will be dad or mum (breast-feeding is a really helpful way of developing a relationship), but it could be another relative or an affectionate carer. The point is that there must be someone able to provide a constant and loving presence.

Attachment theory is sometimes confused with one particular approach to parenting called Attachment Parenting, which advises parents to do everything with their baby, including sleeping together, to ensure the baby bonds. This is not necessary; secure attachments are built through recognizing your baby's unique cues and responding to them with love.

Condensed idea
Your gentle responsiveness now will allow your baby to grow into a secure, emotionally resilient adult

7 Visual playpen

As a newborn, your baby's visual world is quite simple. His undeveloped eyesight means that he sees things in a washed-out blur. This is good, because all that matters is that he can see your face during cuddles and feeds. But there are ways you help his visual skills develop.

A world dimly seen

A newborn baby's eyes are tiny compared to an adult's, even though his head is quite big, and they cannot change their focus much. His eyes see things sharply only when they're about 20–25 cm (8–10 in) away. Anything nearer or further away is blurry. Indeed, an optician would say his vision is about 20/200 or worse – which means he can see at 20 m (65 ft) the detail an adult with normal eyesight can see at 200 m (220 yards). He will learn to focus after about six weeks, but he will remain fairly short-sighted for a long time after.

It's not just focus a newborn's eyes are lacking; he is also unable to make out detail. While an adult can distinguish black and white stripes less than 0.08 mm wide, a six-month-old can only see stripes at least 0.4 mm wide and a newborn can only see stripes more than 3 mm wide.

A newborn baby is also slow to register what he sees. In adults, the nerves that carry visual signals from eye to brain are sheathed in myelin, an electrically insulating material that allows brain signals or impulses to move more quickly. In a baby's brain, the visual nerves haven't yet developed myelin sheaths, so it takes longer for him to 'see' things – that is, to see and recognize that he's looking at something. You will probably notice a slight delay before he responds to any particular sight.

Practising sight

For your baby's visual sense to develop properly, his eyes need stimulation. This is because the more the optical nerves are used, the stronger they become. Visual input also helps the visual part of a baby's brain to grow and develop. However, while gentle stimulation is really valuable, there is a danger of overdoing it, so always remain aware of your baby's responses and take him away from stimulating sights should he show signs of tiredness.

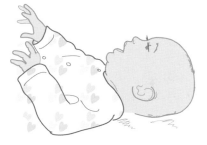

For the first few months of life, your baby won't see the middle of an object nearly as well as the edges, nor will he be able to make out any subtle details. This means that when he gazes up lovingly at you, what he's seeing is mostly your eyes, your hairline and your mouth. That's why toys with simple smiling mouths, dark eyes and a block of colour representing a hairstyle are great, because they remind him of you.

Babies are stimulated by bright colours and can clearly see strong patterns such as stripes, polka dots and checks. Soft pastel variations are lost on babies, but strong patterns excite them. So why not try wearing a bold, stripy shirt every now and then, or hanging a bright check tablecloth on the end of the cot? Some experts recommend stimulating a baby's eyesight through the use of black and white, but provide too much of this to gaze on at once, because an overload of strong patterns (such as high-contrast black and white) could make him agitated and unable to sleep.

> Just bought a gorgeous mobile for baby James, but he seems to love his dad's funny one made of painted bottle caps and shirt buttons! #daddysboy

To help improve your baby's visual focus, try setting out objects within his field of vision in various positions around him. This will give him the chance or incentive to look in different directions. If he seems to face the wall on the same side all the time, using one eye mostly, try moving his cot occasionally, so that he'll need to use a different eye to find his favourite object. And try holding him on alternate sides of your body while feeding.

Variety show

For the first two months, your baby's eyes will not be coordinated, and may even look crossed. It takes a while before they start to work together to judge distance and see movement. He won't reach for things he sees until about 4–6 months of age, which is when he begins to realize that some things are close to him while others are distant.

Movement through the air creates patterns. That's why mobiles and other moving objects are so fascinating for babies. But there's no need to spend lots of money: a home-made mobile with shapes dangling from a coathanger or cardboard ring on cotton thread is just as good, as long as it's delicate enough to ripple and sway in even a gentle breeze. The most important thing is to hang it safely out of your baby's reach.

Don't feel that you have to buy expensive visual stimulants; you can fill your baby's visual world with objects from around the home. Simply collect a range of bold, brightly coloured and patterned things (such as clothes) and present two or three new ones to him every couple of days or so, as a kind of variety show. Hold them up in front of his face, about 20–25 cm (8–10 in) from his eyes, and leave them there long enough for him to explore them visually in his own time. Almost anything will do – clothes, jars, cereal packets, plastic bowls – but things which make a nice noise when moved are especially good. You can also leave a few of them near his cot for a while sometimes – perhaps on a nearby but unreachable table – so he can look at them in his own time. But remember that the most interesting object of all, to him, is your face.

Using movement

One of the most important visual skills a baby learns is how to track movement. You can help him develop this skill by doing the following:

- Hold your baby still, 20–30 cm (8–12 in) in front of your face, then very slowly and gently sway your head from side to side and up and down, so that he has a chance to follow you with his eyes. Then try holding still yourself, and gently moving his body instead.
- Do the same thing with a smiley-faced doll or a soft toy that has a bell attached, so that your baby's eyes follow the sound.
- Arrange a toy above the cot so that it can swing from side to side, and gently push it into action when going to collect your baby after a sleep.

Condensed idea
You can help to develop your baby's eyesight by creating his personal art and design gallery!

8 Smiley face

Perhaps the most Important things in your baby's life are her mum's and dad's faces. Learning to recognize and read these, and, later, other faces, is a crucial part of early intellectual development. Learning to read faces well at this age will help for the rest of her life.

Facial recognition

A few years ago, scientists made a remarkable discovery. It always used to be assumed that babies were born with little knowledge of human faces. They were presumed to be pretty much 'blank slates' on which recognition of faces, starting with their parents, was gradually imprinted.

It now transpires that babies start out with the ability to recognize a wide range of faces – and not just human faces but monkey faces too. But they gradually lose the ability to recognize any faces they do not see in those early days. It's a skill that seems to go by the system 'use it or lose it'.

In one groundbreaking study, two groups of six-month-old babies were shown pictures of the faces of Barbary macaque monkeys. One group was not shown them again, while the other was shown the faces regularly over the next three months. It turned out that the babies who saw the faces regularly had no problem telling the difference between individual monkeys – something even experts working closely with monkeys find tricky. Those babies who saw the faces just once could not see the difference. The same seems true of familiar and unfamiliar human faces. Babies are born with a general idea of what a face is and an ability to make incredibly fine distinctions between different faces. They focus in particular on eyes, nose and mouth. But by the time they are nine months old, they can distinguish differences only between faces they see most often – losing the ability, for instance, to clearly identify the differences between faces of racial types they do not see in these early days. Some scientists believe this specialization is then hard-wired into the brain, but others believe the brain is more plastic and can be opened up again later. The reason for this 'fine-tuning' into familiar faces is that it helps babies develop the ability to recognize tiny differences in facial expressions, which will be very important in dealing with people later in life.

Look at me!

One thing that is clear, though, is that babies are very good at recognizing their own mothers. One study presented videos of women to babies just 12–36 hours old – and they all showed a clear preference for seeing their own mother's face rather than the faces of strangers. It's evident that for a baby, seeing a parent's face – the person on whom

Newborn empathy

One of the strange things about visiting a ward full of newborns is that if one of them starts to cry, they all start crying! In the same way that babies seem to enjoy 'jokes' with their parents (by smiling when their parents laugh), studies have shown that newborn babies can also empathize with other newborns. They cry for longer and more pitifully when they hear another newborn cry, as though picking up on the emotion, but with a clear sense that the other baby is separate from themselves. Psychologists have hypothesized that babies may do this 'herd crying' to send out an alarm that attention is needed.

they depend for survival – is really, really important. Newborns like people who make eye contact; people who look at them (without staring hard) hold their interest much more than people who don't. And babies become distressed if caregivers don't look at them very much. Humans are social animals right from the start and they really need this face-to-face engagement. Your face is much, much better than any mobile or patterns at boosting your baby's brain. So although it's good to give her interesting objects to look at, don't skimp on 'face time' with your baby either. When she is 0–6 months old, one of her favourite things will simply be the sight of her mum's or dad's face, around 30 cm (12 in) away, so just by lying down beside her, your faces close together, you'll be reassuring your baby and helping her development in all sorts of ways.

> Have discovered that Milly is fine with a nappy change as long as I make silly faces while doing it! #slapstickmum

Your face or mine?

Amazingly, newborns can mimic human expressions right from the start. Research has shown that when newborns are shown videos of strangers pulling faces, they quickly start to mimic them. And of course, your face is the one your baby will really love to follow and imitate. That's why it's so important to give your baby face time – playing facial games (pulling different expressions, opening and closing your eyes, sticking out your tongue and so on) – but above all, smiling at her, because it's absolutely clear that smiling makes a baby happiest. And don't underestimate the power of your smile – practising smiling and recognizing smiles is crucial for early brain development.

The ability to mimic suggests that babies can link the way a face looks to how a person feels on the inside. That's why your happy face is so good for her; she senses that you are happy in her presence, so the

bond between you is strong and reliable. You can experiment with your baby's ability to 'read' your facial expressions. Choose a time when she is relaxed and alert, then try pulling faces and see how she responds. She won't be able to see your expressions very clearly when she's very young, so make them really big and exaggerated, but always friendly. Stick out your tongue or make a silly yawn. It may be that it's not just because your gestures are big that she likes them, but because they make you laugh, and that pleases her, too. There's every chance that she will enjoy the joke if you do. With each new face you pull, give your baby a couple of minutes to try imitating it before you move on to the next one. Remember to look for any signs of overstimulation that should signal an end to your game.

Condensed idea
Spending 'face time' with your baby helps her learn how to read expressions

9 Soundtracks

A newborn baby's world is a world of sound. Even when he's lying on his back in the dark, or snuggling against mum to feed or dad for a cuddle, he hears sounds all the time. You can help the aural pathways develop by keeping him provided with a rich array of sounds.

Listening before birth

Hearing is one of the first senses to develop. Physically, a baby's ears are fully formed in the womb by early in the third trimester of pregnancy, and there is evidence that he hears a lot of sounds echoing through to his dark cocoon. He hears his mum's heartbeat, of course, and the gurgling of her digestive system. But he probably hears the sound of his mum's voice both from inside and outside, and maybe he hears, too, the voice of his dad and other family members, which is surely why these sounds will always mean so much to him.

Research has shown that many newborn babies can recognize their mother's and even their father's voices (if he's been chatting to the 'bump' during pregnancy). And, of course, much has been made of music that appears to filter through to a baby in the womb (see page 19) and is recognized by the baby after birth.

It certainly seems likely that in the womb a baby does begin to learn to distinguish between different sounds, which means that the aural pathways in his little brain are already beginning to develop by the time he emerges into the world. Physically, most babies' hearing is as good as an average adult, though he may not hear quieter ambient sounds at first. Of course, a tiny minority of babies do have hearing problems, but hospitals can pick up on this with simple tests. What newborns can't do, however, is clearly differentiate between sounds and understand what they mean.

Gradually, though, as a baby hears particular sounds repeated, they strengthen aural pathways in the brain, and as these are reinforced, they begin to have more meaning for him. This is an important and necessary part of learning how to make sense of the world of sounds around, and in particular human speech. But, of course, the opposite process is also true – aural pathways for sounds he hears less often become weakened. That's why it helps to keep your baby's sound world rich and varied – and you can also help him begin to make sense of sounds and figure out their meaning. If you shake a carton of rice, for instance, look at both it and him, so he begins to understand what's making the sound.

> My baby's favourite game is banging a metal bowl on the wall of the cot. It drives me nuts, but he loves it! #mypoorears

Chatterbox

Of course, babies will learn about sounds even if they're left to their own devices, but they'll learn more readily if someone gives them a helping hand. One of the best ways to do this is to keep your baby with you while you're doing things. If you have a sling, carry him with you while you're doing the vacuuming, chopping vegetables or typing an email. If a sling is not feasible, simply prop him up or lay him down nearby, so that he can become familiar with all these household sounds.

But don't forget that his favourite sound by far is your voice. So while you're going about your daily tasks or changing his nappy, keep up a running commentary. Chatter away in a happy voice, and tell him about anything you like, from what you're going to buy at the shops to

Music making

You'll soon find that after a few months babies love making noise – it's one great big game. And as long as you can take it, it's great to encourage him by giving him things to make noises with:

- Rattles are just a start – the noisier and more brightly coloured the better.
- Anything that makes a sound is great – try a plastic bottle filled with dried peas or a ball with a bell in it.
- At about six months of age, your baby can start to bang things as well as shake them.
- Toy drums are great fun, but a wooden spoon and a saucepan are just as good.
- Encourage your baby to shout along as you sing and beat out a rhythm together.

how tricky it is to clean the pans and how the economy is going down the drain. In fact, it doesn't matter at all what you say; the important thing is for him to hear your voice. Don't forget to take a break; gentle talk-radio can be a good temporary substitute.

It's not just the variations in sounds that matter but their direction, too. It takes quite a while for a baby to learn how to pinpoint sound. So play little games with him to help him develop this sense, by encouraging him to work out where your voice is coming from. Start by saying something when you're close to him and he's looking at you. Then try calling his name softly from a little further away, or higher up or lower. Each time, give him a little time to turn his gaze and see where you're calling from. Don't overdo it and always keep it fun.

Rattles and bells

It doesn't just have to be your voice, of course. Toys and objects that make a noise, such as a rattling matchbox or a set of keys, can be just as much fun. Just move them around and see if he can turn his head to see them. Encourage him by turning your face to look at the noise, too.

From about six weeks on, your baby will begin to learn that he can make sounds too. Noisy toys are easier for him to find than silent ones, and he will gradually work out that he can actually make them jingle and rattle himself. Rattles and little bells are great, of course, but at an early stage when he's only just beginning to move you could try musical mittens. They were originally developed long ago for infants with poor hand–eye coordination, but they make a great game for younger babies.

You can make your own 'bell mittens' by sewing a little bell or two very firmly inside the tips of each mitt (sew them inside so that he can't injure himself with them). As he moves his hand and jingles the bell, his gaze will turn to see the source of the sound – and eventually he'll realize it is him making the sound as he moves his hand! Try a mitt on the right hand first, then the left, and eventually both together.

Condensed idea
A rich array of sounds will help your baby's aural pathways develop

10 A feel of the world

Of all your baby's senses, touch is the earliest to develop and the most fundamental. Touch sensors grow along with nerve cells within a few weeks of conception and when your baby is born her ability to understand her surroundings begins with tactile sensations.

Learning at a lick

As every parent knows, when a young baby gets hold of something for the first time, she'll often put it in her mouth straightaway to try it out. That's of course why everything you give her must be clean and impossible to swallow. But she's not doing this just to be awkward or because she's obsessed with eating. She's doing it to learn.

Touch, or feeling, is how a newborn learns about things, and at this stage in her life the densest and most sensitive nerve endings are in her tongue. Evidence suggests that a one-month-old baby can form an abstract mental image of something they've just sucked on, which is something they can't do with their hands at this stage. So don't try to stop her putting things in her mouth; she's exploring! In fact, the more things you allow her to try out this way the better. All you need to do is ensure they're safe for this oral learning process.

When you want to introduce your baby to a new object, don't just show it to her – give it to her to feel with her hands and even her feet. You could start looking for things for her to explore with her hands and feet from just a few weeks old. Give her things with a whole variety of textures. Things that are hard, like a wooden spoon. Things that are soft, like a teddy bear. Things that are squidgy like a sponge. Things that are

crunchy like paper. Things that are smooth or rough, warm or cold, furry or silky, firm or giving, and so on. Every new texture will be added to the memory bank.

The power of touch

Although nerve endings are densest in the tongue, hands and feet, there are touch sensors all over a baby's body. The skin is our largest and most fundamental sense organ. It has thousands of receptors that are uniquely able to stimulate the brain. That's why it's good to keep the house warm enough to leave your baby naked every now and then, or dressed occasionally in just a loose dress or vest. This allows her to explore the materials with all or most of her body.

Numerous studies and experiments, on both human and animal babies, have shown that the way a baby is touched, even in its first few hours, has a huge impact on its neurological development and coping strategies as an adult. A century ago, many babies in orphanages died before they were seven months old. This was attributed to marasmus, meaning 'wasting away' – the babies failed to thrive because no one was picking them up or cuddling them. It's for this reason that hospitals today ensure that babies in special-care units are given a massage several times a day, and often picked up by a volunteer and rocked.

Baby massage

Skin-to-skin contact with your baby is vital. For the first six weeks and beyond, your baby needs to be held, rocked, caressed and physically reassured as often as feels right. Try giving her a massage every now

Getting a grip

At first, many of a baby's movements are reflexes rather than deliberate, but this changes as the baby grows:

- **0–2 months:** the grasp reflex is present at birth, and a baby will instinctively grip another person's finger if it touches her palm.
- **3 months:** a baby can begin to grip things more deliberately and swat them with her hand. This is a good time to let a baby lie on the floor with things to bat about.
- **4–8 months:** most babies are able to pick up larger objects such as blocks, but not smaller things. They put many objects straight to their mouths for testing. This means it's a time to watch your baby like a hawk!
- **9–12 months:** this is the stage that babies develop the pincer grip between thumb and fingers, allowing them to pick up smaller things and maybe even hold a spoon. Some babies begin to show a preference for left or right hand at this age.

and then. Make sure the room is really warm before you start, then take off your baby's clothes and nappy and lay her on a towel. Rub a little baby oil on your hands, then start by wrapping your hands round one of her thighs and gently pulling your hands down to her feet (as though you're 'milking' her legs). Follow this with a little foot massage, tracing circles on the soles of her feet with your thumbs.

> Baby massage at bedtime is turning out to be a great way for us to relax together – and it seems to help her sleep better. #gentledad

Then use the 'milking' technique on her arms, pulling gently from the top of her arms to her wrists, before starting to massage her hands, by tracing circles on her palms. This will almost certainly make her smile! Massage her chest by placing your hands side by side on it, then gently stroking outwards (repeat this several times). Roll her on to her tummy, and massage her back using the palms of your hands, working from her shoulder blades down towards her bottom. Finish by running your hands from her shoulders right down to her feet. Then wrap her up in some warm clothes and give her a cuddle. She's likely to be so relaxed that she'll probably want to doze off.

Body contact keeps your baby calm and chemically well balanced (it reduces levels of the stress hormone, cortisol) and this allows brain pathways to develop in peace. This means that the brain grows healthily and your baby feels serene. It will also help you to develop the bond that is such a vital part of her wellbeing. Loving touch is essential.

Condensed idea
Touch is the most primitive and vital of a baby's senses, so give her lots of shapes and textures to explore

(11) Food for thought

Great claims are made for some foods being superfoods that can help build a super-brain. Such claims are hard to prove, but there is no doubt that some foods are vital for general health – and a healthy baby is a baby with the energy to learn and develop to his full potential.

Mother's milk

In recent decades, 'breast is best' has become such a mantra in the affluent west that some people have reacted against it, wondering if they are being brainwashed. The validity of earlier research that seemed to show that breast milk boosted IQ has come under question, because affluent mothers may be more likely to follow the advice to breast-feed, and some have suggested that the better performance of breast-fed babies owes more to their comfortable lifestyle than to mother's milk.

However, the weight of evidence has built up. In 2012, for instance, a major study by Arkansas Children's Nutrition Center showed that while babies fed on milk formula, soy formula and breast milk all had normal brain development, breast-fed babies outscored both groups of formula-fed babies in their mental development and their ability to combine cognitive function and physical movement. The difference wasn't large but it was measurable. Another study published in November 2012 showed observably better development in key areas of the brain for babies fed exclusively on breast milk.

No one yet knows what it is in breast milk that helps brain development and some scientists suggest it may not actually be the milk that matters at all, but the process of breast-feeding, as the bonding stimulates the release of the hormone oxytocin. A lot of people, though, believe that a fatty acid known as docosahexaenoic acid (DHA) is involved. DHA and another fatty acid known as ARA (arachidonic acid) seem to be important in visual development in babies and speed up nerve transmission. The body can't make much of these fatty acids itself – but they are found in breast milk, and are now added to some formula milks. They are also present in salmon and tuna, liver and eggs and seaweed, which is good to bear in mind as your baby grows.

Substances to avoid

Some substances that may be used in packaging or found on non-organic food can be harmful to children and their development, and should be avoided:

- PVC is a plastic that can be toxic for young babies, but is often used in soft children's products.
- Pesticides, especially organophosphates, are dangerous for babies because they block the action of enzymes that control muscle action.
- Mercury can damage an infant's concentration and learning ability – so avoid mercury thermometers, fluorescent lights with mercury, and paints with mercury (most paint is now lead- and mercury-free).
- Lead impairs mental development. It is sometimes found in paint, batteries, toys, ceramics and even tap water, where this enters the home through old lead pipes. If you're stuck with lead pipes, run the tap for several minutes each time before you use the water.
- Solvents: there are many solvents that release toxic fumes, so check for this carefully before you use any in the house.

Whatever the direct benefits for your baby's brain, few people now doubt that breast milk is immensely beneficial for general health. Study after study has shown that breast milk is a great source of vitamins, minerals, proteins and essential fats, and that it boosts a baby's immune system, as it includes the mother's antibodies (this is important for many reasons, not least because a sick child will find it harder to progress intellectually). A typical recommendation is breast milk alone for the first 4–6 months and then breast milk supplemented by solids for the next six and perhaps beyond. However, every baby and mother is different, and some mothers find breast-feeding genuinely distressing – if this remains the case even after seeking medical help, it makes no sense to persist. Formulas have improved hugely in recent years and can be a good source of nutrients, and the happiness of the mother and baby during feeding will more than make up for any nutritional deficiencies.

> My local café reserves a private area for breastfeeding mums – it's packed out by 10 a.m.! #feedmenow

Solid food for the brain

Once your baby is on solid foods, the most important thing is to offer him a nutritious, balanced diet to ensure he stays healthy. The greater the nutritional value of your baby's food, the greater the size of his caudate – that's the part of the brain that specializes in learning and memory. Aim for a good balance of fruit and vegetables, whole grains and lean meat. In the UK, the NHS provides online guidance on baby meals and nutrition, and there are lots of parenting websites with great ideas for recipes.

For brain development, there are two substances that may be especially valuable in your baby's diet. The first is omega-3 fatty acids (including DHA). Apart from breast milk, omega-3s are most plentiful in foods that

should only be introduced gradually to a baby's diet, such as fish, leafy green vegetables and eggs. Fish such as salmon, tuna and sardines are rich in fatty acids, but some babies can have allergic reactions to fish, and you must be ultra-careful to avoid bones. Leafy green vegetables are rich in fatty acids, too, but don't introduce them too soon – the nitrates in them can be converted by very young babies' bodies to nitrites, which reduce the blood's ability to carry oxygen. Eggs, too, are a great food from about ten months on but use the yolks only and hard-boil them.

The second element is iron, which is vital for making haemoglobin (the molecule that carries oxygen in the blood). Babies have enough stored iron for the first six months, but then need to absorb it from food. Formula milk is enriched with iron, but breast-fed babies may need to get iron through foods such as fortified baby cereals, chicken liver, beef, chicken, tofu or egg yolks. Very few babies in western countries suffer from anaemia, but always check with your doctor if you have any concerns.

Condensed idea
Healthy food provides the building blocks for brain and muscle development

12 I did that!

A baby very gradually learns that she can make things happen in the world: she can turn her head to see where a sound is coming from, or grip things with her hands and pull them towards her. You can help her make these links between her actions and the world.

Born to learn

Psychology professor Alison Gopnik has argued very persuasively that children are born experimenters. Almost from the moment they are born they are trying things out with all the intent of a scientist. It's clear that even at three months old, a baby can tell that she can make things happen in the real world and is delighted to do so. Gopnik cites a simple demonstration that you can do for yourself. Just tie one end of a ribbon to one of your baby's feet, and the other to a mobile. Tie it loosely so there's some slack, but so her leg movement will cause the mobile to move. She'll soon discover that the mobile shakes around when she kicks her foot. She may be so delighted that her experiment works that she starts smiling and cooing as she shakes her foot energetically to see the mobile moving.

Then try tying the ribbon to her foot so that it doesn't move the mobile, or move the mobile on its own, without using the ribbon. You'll notice that she thinks it's not nearly so much fun. You'll soon see that what excites her is trying something out and finding she can make it happen. She may not yet have worked out just why it happens or what the connection is. She may even try smiling at the mobile to make it move, which is quite logical when you think that if she smiles at you, you move – so in her mind smiles have the power to make things move.

Scientist at play

The Swiss psychologist Jean Piaget was one of the first people to systematically study cognitive development – the way that our thinking develops. He showed that by the time they are one year old, babies really are trying systematically to work out how the world works. Look at a little infant playing for a while and you'll see it's not quite as random and chaotic as it appears. In fact, a one-year-old baby is often more systematic in her play experiments than many a scientist. Watch a baby banging a brick for instance – as often as not you can see her trying different things out to see their effect. She may bang the brick hard at first. Then softly. Then she might try dropping it. Or flinging it down. She's not just testing one hypothesis – she's testing several at the same time. She's conducting experiments, analyzing the results, and forming theories about the physical world and her interaction with it.

If you think of this play as an experiment rather than just random fun, you'll begin to appreciate just how valuable it is to her growing understanding of the world. You'll even see her stop every now and then as if to process what her experiments have told her so far. This curiosity is a drive as natural and powerful as the need to sleep and eat – and this is why play is such a crucial part of learning and brain development.

Play is finding out about the world, trying different things, seeing how they work and which things don't work. For most infants, it is among the most pleasurable of all activities. That's why it's important to provide a rich array of opportunities for your junior scientist to experiment. All you have to do is give her things to play with. When she's able to move around, make sure her curiosity doesn't lead her into all kinds of dangerous scrapes (such as sticking her fingers into electric sockets).

The world in her hands

Active exploration really begins at around 3–4 months of age. This is when a baby begins to learn to control her arms – to be able to move them consciously and purposefully. Gradually, she also learns that she can use her arms to reach out to things – like cuddly toys or your arm –

A home-made baby gym

Not all babies realize that they can make things happen, so why not help your baby to find out? One of the easiest ways to do this is to tie some toys onto something stable so they hang down just in front of your baby. Place them at a distance that allows her to hit them if she reaches out. A toy that makes a rewarding noise when touched is best. Sit behind her and gently guide her hands towards the toy, making sure you guide both her hands towards the toy, not just one. Remember at all times to keep it fun – babies learn by playing.

though for a while she may not be able to do anything more than flap and touch these objects by chance. You can gently help her by turning her towards a desired object – such as her favourite teddy – and guiding her little hands towards it. Give her lots to think and wonder about, to encourage this curiosity.

Dangle a few objects in front of her (see box, facing page) or put her under a shop-bought baby 'gym' to encourage her to try reaching and touching. Talk to her as

> My scientist baby loves his bouncy chair. You should see his delight when he sways and the chair moves! #babyeinstein

she's playing, and make encouraging noises. If you have a bouncing cradle chair, take the opportunity to attach moving things to it, such as springy toys and mobiles. That way she's not only encouraged to reach out, but will see things move as she moves in the bouncer – and she may realize that it is her movement that makes them move. She will find this especially thrilling, which is exactly the kind of emotion that will motivate her to keep experimenting.

Gripping is at first a reflex action over which a baby has no control (she will grip your finger from an early stage). But gradually your baby will realize that she can move both hands together and hold things with them, and that she can uncurl her fingers and use them to grip, too. This is an exciting discovery, that will lead your baby to new levels of experimentation. Later she will learn to grasp objects and (from around 6–8 months of age) will realize she can pull them towards her. Importantly, she's learned that she can make things happen, and make changes in the world she sees. That's when the fun really begins.

Condensed idea
Babies learn by experiment that they can make things happen in the world

13 Brain on the move

After your baby is born, he gradually learns to control his body movements, discovering everything from how to grip things to how to walk. These 'motor skills' are not simply physical – they both promote and are profoundly influenced by brain development.

Motoring along

Motor skills are essentially muscle movements and there are two kinds: gross motor skills and fine motor skills. Gross motor skills involve the bigger, stronger muscles, such as those in the legs and arms. They're the skills that enable a baby to, progressively, hold his head up, sit, crawl, walk, run, jump and skip. Fine motor skills are the small movements of the hands, fingers and toes – the skills that enable a baby to pick things up with his fingers, hold something steadily, or guide something to a particular place. Fine motor skills in particular are tied into brain development, progressing with cognitive, visual and social development.

When a baby is born, he has very little control over his movements. But gradually his motor skills spread through his body, starting with the head and moving down and out to include his neck and shoulders, then moving out through his torso and into his limbs. He'll learn to control his arms and legs before he can control his hands and feet.

Gross motor skills

The gross motor skills develop through the first year or so in recognizable stages, though each baby reaches them at different ages. At each stage you can help your baby gently along the way. As he gets older, move him

Milestones in motor skills

Here are some of the milestones your baby will pass, and some ideas for helping him achieve them more easily:

• **Head control:** for the first three months or so, you need to support your baby's head because he can't do it himself. Only after about seven months will he be able to hold his head steady and upright while sitting on your lap. It's a gradual process. Begin with some gentle neck exercises that encourage him to lift his head – by making silly noises at his feet, or holding a favourite toy just above his chest. Later, he'll be able to lift his head from the ground. Encourage this by laying him on a soft spot on the floor, then bring your face close to his – move your head around so that his head follows you.

• **Rolling over:** around four or five months (or later), you'll suddenly find your baby can roll over for himself. Usually it's only in one direction for a while (stomach to back or vice versa) and it will probably take a few months more for him to learn how to roll both ways. Give him plenty of time to roll about on a soft, clean floor. Help and praise him as he tries, and always make it a game. Hold a toy or a rattle to encourage him to turn, but be ready to end the game as soon as he shows signs of tiredness.

• **Sitting up:** this often follows on not far behind rolling and it's a huge breakthrough, because now your baby can see the world properly for himself. Sit him on your lap facing out so he begins to enjoy the view, with as little support as you feel safe and comfortable with. Then try propping him up on cushions on the floor as you watch closely.

from the cot to the floor, or from his tummy onto his back, and encourage him to do little exercises like push-ups from his tummy or reaching for a toy when he's upright. You can help him, too, by showing him what to do: try moving his arms and legs like a bicycle, or pulling him up to a sitting position. Keep it fun and never overdo it, so he doesn't get tired.

Fine motor skills

Fine motor skills take longer to develop, but they are the ones that create the most connections in the brain. The more detailed and controlled they are, the more extensive the connections – because, of course, moving fingers in a controlled way is not just about fine muscle movements, it's about exploration, visual coordination, intentional interaction with the world and much more.

In the first three months, your baby will follow bright objects with his eyes, and may even turn his head to follow voices. By three months he may be smiling at faces. Encourage him to explore with his hands by bringing them to your face. Noisy soft toys with handles thin enough for a baby to hold are great for encouraging motor skills. Later, as your baby begins to sit up and grasp things, place toys in enticing positions and encourage him to look from one to another by setting them a little way apart – in the bath, on the cot wall and so on. Put things on your face or mouth such as plastic sunglasses and silly hats and encourage him to pull them off. Releasing things is just as important as grasping them, so encourage him

> My seven-month-old loves pulling pasta apart. Brilliant finger exercise! #fingerfood

to drop toys in the bath to make a satisfying splash. Once he can roll over and really grasp things with both hands, give him lots of things he can bang and make a noise with, such as spoons and trays and wristbands with bells. Help him learn to use each hand separately by giving him lots of things so small that he can only hold them in one hand, such as soft cereal, cooked pasta and so on, introducing them straight to his hand. Each little skill he learns will build connections in his brain.

Walking tall

Every parent waits anxiously for baby's first steps. A typical time is about one year old, but babies can start as early as nine months or later than 16 months with no noticeable effect on general development. This is certainly not something to worry about. Researchers have found that walking is not simply a matter of balance, strength and coordination; it is a question of temperament, too. Active, impulsive children tend to learn to walk early, while more thoughtful children tend to walk later.

Condensed idea
Each motor skill your baby learns will build connections in his brain

(14) Facing the world

Some parents treat their babies almost as if they are sickly patients, lying them down with a view of practically nothing but the ceiling. But you can give your baby's brain development a real boost by offering her opportunities to see the world more often.

Baby brains need input!

A growing baby's brain needs input: new sights, new experiences and new data to process. These are all mental fodder to help develop brain connections and help your baby build a picture of the world. Although you don't want to expose him to a world so full of new experiences and stimulations that he gets tired and fractious, there's no doubt that a rich variety of sights and sounds will do more for him than a sterile, unchanging outlook. This is the time when unused pathways in the brain wither away (whereas 'cells that fire together, wire together', forming strong associations that help memory and learning), so there are many benefits to enriching a baby's experiences at this stage.

> Turns out that carrying my baby upright in a baby carrier stops him possetting, as well as giving him a better view! #sherpamum

It's not hard to do this. You don't need to get him all kinds of brain-boosting toys and gimmicks. All you need to do is give him the chance to see the world around him. Place him in an active part of the home where things are going on, so he can see them and hear them.

Some parents are tempted to lay babies down somewhere quiet and out of the way to keep them calm. That's fine if it's time for them to sleep. But if a baby is wide awake, why not sit him up somewhere he can see lots of activity? If you're doing the ironing, for instance, prop him up safely with some cushions or in a bouncy chair so that he can watch what's going on. Talk to him frequently to keep him engaged, of course, but let him also just enjoy the sights and sounds every now and then. However familiar they are to you, they are entirely new to him. Just keep an eye out for when he's tired – your responsiveness to his signals is essential for his continuing sense of attachment (see pages 24–27).

A seat with a view

Wherever you are, think about where you sit your baby down. Whether you're visiting friends, doing stuff at home or sitting in a café, put your baby in a position where there's lots to look at. If there's a suitable window, sit him so he can see out and watch the trees swaying in the

Visual delights

Babies are ready to learn different things at different times,
and they also delight in different things at different ages.
Babies of 2–6 months old like to be held close, and love it
when you put your face close to theirs (about 30 cm/12 in)
away). From 7–12 months, babies like to look at
their own reflection in the mirror and pat it. They
may also stare at things for long periods, trying to
figure them out, and they love to look at books.
As they gain a sense of independence, at around
one year old, they develop feelings of empathy
towards others, and like watching and then
imitating other people's actions. At this age babies
will point to things in books and to interesting
things around them.

garden or people walking down the street. In a café, give him the seat
which faces onto all the people and the service area. For him, these
sights will be as good as a TV documentary or a trip to the theatre. When
you go out for a walk, carry him in a sling facing outwards so he can see
what's going on. Sometimes, he will need to feel safe and secure against
your body, facing inwards, but if he's in the mood, turn him round so he
can see the changing scenery.

Pram or pushchair?

It's worth thinking about how you transport your baby, too. Ideally,
his transport should give him a good view of the world and allow
free movement while he's awake – but also provide a safe, snug place
to sleep. Traditional prams are great for sleeping, but they provide

a restricted view of the world when he's awake. Some car seats, on the other hand, give him a good view when he's awake, but can be uncomfortable when he's tired – and even slightly dangerous if he slumps forward so that his breathing is restricted. When you're buying a pushchair, look for one that allows your baby to sit up or recline progressively. Some pushchairs (unfortunately the more expensive types) carry your baby at waist height. That's great for you, as it means you don't have to bend down as far – and it's great for him too, because he'll be at table height, where all the action is going on. It means your baby will be closer to your face and arms too, which he'll like.

Babies and backpacks

Many parents like to use baby carriers and soft slings. The great thing about these is that they ensure maximum bonding time for younger babies (who feel secure snuggled up next to the carrying parent) while also providing baby with a constantly changing view. Young babies can be carried in either front- or back-fitting slings; you might like to progress from front to back, which will give your growing baby the freedom to look around and over your shoulder. Front-facing carriers allow older babies to have a brilliantly unrestricted view and the potential for good interaction with people. Sturdy baby backpack carriers are made to carry babies from six months old, and some of these even come with a rain hood and sun canopy, so your baby can enjoy a great, high-up view.

Baby carriers also make it easier for you to get out and about, which is good for you and your baby. A carrier will also leave both your hands free to do things. Most parents find that slings and backpacks give them and their baby a sense of freedom that both find stimulating and fun.

Condensed idea
Babies learn by looking, so make sure you give your baby a good view of the world

15 Like me, like you

Babies learn many things through imitation. Adults use it instinctively, smiling when someone else smiles, for instance. But for a baby, making faces with you isn't just fun – it's a key part of her discovery of who she is and how she can interact with the world.

I see you

There are times when you pick up your baby and gaze into her eyes, and it's sheer delight. She gazes back into your eyes. She smiles at you. You smile back. She makes an odd face. You copy her, with a smile in your eyes. It's a great game, a great moment of bonding and an important learning experience for your baby – because copycat interaction is

crucial for her. She sees from the way you try to mimic her that she is understood. As she sees you reflecting her expressions, she learns that she can have an effect on the world.

Facial mimicking is an early part of developing communication and social skills, probably the most important skills of all for a baby to learn. It's a great help for you, too, because by watching her expressions and mimicking them, you'll get a closer understanding of how she's thinking and feeling.

Experts have come to call this to-and-fro mimicry 'mirroring'. The term is used as a scientific description of the general process – a process that all of us often employ naturally – and as a name for a simple game you can play with your baby.

The process of mirroring reinforces that all-important bond which is vital for a child's self-confidence (see pages 24–27). It also helps a child to organize her feelings as she sees them mirrored in your expressions, enabling her to develop appropriate responses to the world. What kind of expression do you make when she frowns? What does your face do when a dog barks? Or when your baby cries? Your tiny scientist is watching you and learning all the time, and this kind of interaction measurably stimulates nerve growth

> Annie and gramps playing mirroring games – lots of funny faces and giggles. #busymum

and the emotional circuits in the brain, as it encourages the release of chemicals such as opioids, endorphins and oxytocin in the brain. As parents and other significant carers mirror a baby, they become more attuned to each other, which in itself reassures and calms a baby. Mirroring has even been shown to reduce tantrums.

Play the game

Mirroring is a great game you can play with a child of literally any age, but it's especially effective with young babies. When she's in a lively, alert mood, set her down at eye level, facing you, and explain that you're going to copy her. Of course, she won't understand quite what you mean, but the ritual helps establish that this is for her, too. Now watch her and copy her every movement, whether it's smiling, blinking or waving a hand. Keep eye contact, and show her she's doing well. Mimic sounds, too, such as coos and burbles. Don't go on for more than a few minutes without checking that she's happy and wants to go on longer. And always keep it positive; praise her when you see even the faintest flicker of a response, to show her that her efforts have been understood. Make it a two-way process, where sometimes you lead the way with a silly sound or weird expression, while at other times she leads and you follow, always keeping a gentle rhythm and approach.

The great thing is that mum, dad, grandparents, aunts, uncles and family friends can all try mirroring with your baby. In this way, she will get to know everyone who's important in her life and will gradually learn what different facial expressions mean. Mirroring also helps newborns focus and track things with their eyes. As you practise with your baby, she'll gradually get more and more confident in leading, and may well enjoy this game for quite a few years.

Taking turns

Learning to take turns is so natural that parents and babies go through it without thinking of it as anything but a fun game. But it's an important step in learning how to interact with people and it's the beginnings of the art of conversation. Try doing the following to start a 'conversation' with your baby:

- When you see her looking at you with a blank face, try to start a conversation with a wink or a smile.
- If she responds by moving an eyebrow or moving her head, respond in the same way.
- Give her time to make the next move, so that a dialogue begins to start.
- Build up the responses so they become larger or longer-lasting – always leaving her plenty of time to work out her response.
- Finish the conversation with a big hug and kiss.

That's me!

Most babies seem to love mirrors. Give a baby a mirror and she'll spend hours looking at it and laughing. She may even begin to talk to herself in the mirror. Babies love faces, and her own face in a mirror is endlessly fascinating, and a great source of amusement. Put an unbreakable mirror in her cot, or near where she plays, so she can look whenever she wants. You'll see her begin to notice it more and more.

You can play games with mirrors, too. Sit her on your lap with both of you facing a mirror (close enough for her to see clearly). Then try touching her chin or stroking her arm, or waving her hand – looking all the while in the mirror and encouraging her to do the same and see her reflection waving back. Make sure she knows this is a game – have fun with it, but remember to stop if she shows any signs of tiredness. Dad can even play a game of peek-a-boo by covering the mirror with a cloth every now and then, to make the mum and baby in the mirror vanish, then magically reappear again.

It will take a surprisingly long time, though, for her to realize that the reflection is actually her. It's a big step for her to imagine herself in someone else's place. For a while she may just think her reflection is an entertaining playmate, though, of course, we have no way of knowing. Some researchers test for self-awareness by dabbing a coloured spot of lipstick or blusher on a baby's face. If she touches it or rubs it off after looking in the mirror, she must be self-aware, they conclude. Most infants can't pass this test until they're at least 18 months old. Until then, a mirror is just a hugely entertaining and magical plaything.

Condensed idea
Mirroring is a great way for a baby to learn she is understood and to develop her own understanding of others

16 Joined-up thinking

In the last decade there's been an explosion of research into the developing brain, helped by new scanning techniques that allow researchers to monitor the brain in action. It has confirmed that humans are social animals and that the brain is a social organ.

The interactive brain

The importance of attachment to a baby's wellbeing was recognized long ago through observation of behaviour with primary caregivers (see pages 24–27), but what very recent research has done is delve right inside the developing brain and discover what's going on in terms of brain structure and chemistry. It has shown that not only attachment but all human interactions and emotional responses intricately affect the development of the brain, right down to the level of individual neurons. Emotional response and brain development are completely inseparable.

This marks a profound shift in our understanding. We used to think that we were aware of social connections and could feel empathy for others because we have clever brains – but scientists have realized that in fact, we have clever brains because we develop social connections and empathy. Our brains develop in interaction with other brains, which is why your baby's interaction with you and other people she meets is so crucial to building intelligence.

Some of a baby's brain development is down to genetics and nature, growing independently of any bonding experience and enabling her to learn to eat, walk and be aware. But neurons in the limbic region – the core of the brain that drives the emotions and sense of self – are not fully connected at birth. They develop and make connections only through the loving nurture of parents and caregivers. That's why these early experiences are so vital. There is mounting evidence to show that the brains of babies who are not well-nurtured are distorted in their development, leaving them ill-equipped to deal with the world as they grow up. If that sounds depressing, there is also the recent encouraging discovery of the brain's 'neural plasticity' – its ability to constantly change and make new connections and even new neurons throughout life. It was once thought that our brain circuitry became fixed early on in life, and degenerated as we aged. However neuroscience has shown that brain connections are constantly remoulded by experience and interactions, and some of the damage caused by poor nurture early on may actually be repaired by later receiving huge amounts of loving care.

The whole brain comes into play

The bridge between the two halves of your baby's brain, known as the corpus callosum, begins to develop at about 12 months of age. This is when the benefits of secure attachment really begin to pay off, as the different parts of the brain begin to become integrated in a way that only good nurturing can promote. The brain begins to function as a whole in the following ways:

- The deeper brain feeds emotional experiences to the higher brain, which attaches meaning and suggests a response; this happens in self-soothing.
- The right- and left-brain share feelings and thoughts, providing an ever-shifting balance of holism (whole body experience) and detail. The more integrated a baby's brain, the better it works.

The power of fear

A strong two-way bond between parent and baby is necessary for survival – it ensures the baby's protection and safety in times of danger. Ultimately all babies begin to explore their surroundings, but exploration inevitably leads at times to a fearful situation. This triggers the need for reassurance from the attachment figure (see pages 24–27), before the baby feels secure enough for further exploration. The process starts with fear; parental encouragement then soothes the fear; and this provides the baby with the confidence to start exploring again.

Fear is what drives the instant 'fight, flight or freeze' response that is controlled by the deeper, older regions of the brain, and in particular the small brain organ known as the amygdala. This reacts in just 200 milliseconds – whereas it takes 3–5 seconds for situations to register in the cortex, the conscious part of the brain. In fact, 80 per cent of the time, our amygdala responds to and stores an experience in our unconscious memory without us ever being aware of it. Research has shown that the brain structures which allow conscious processing of emotional relationships are not mature until they are 2½–3 years old. So all those earlier experiences of attachment are stored only unconsciously – they're all processed by the amygdala. In fact, it seems emotional experiences and patterns of attachment settle lastingly in your baby's brain in those first 12–18 months without her being aware. It's only after she's 18 months old that she'll be able to explicitly, consciously process experiences and relationships and so begin to remember them.

Brain chemistry

Hormones seem to play a key part in emotional regulation – the ability to soothe oneself in times of fear or stress. The key hormone is oxytocin, which is triggered through the gentle touch of another human being, such as stroking. It calms the amygdala (which reacts fast and unconsciously), and as the baby grows, it stimulates the links between the amygdala and the cortex, providing rational feedback on an experience. This is why hugs and kisses make a baby feel safe – they trigger the release of a soothing bath of oxytocin. The reaction between acts of love and oxytocin becomes so powerful that even memories can trigger a release of this soothing hormone.

> Turns out I'm not just losing grey cells after all – my brain is still developing just like my baby's! #oldermum

The human brain has two halves, or hemispheres, and the pre-frontal cortex develops differently in each half of the brain. From 0–18 months, the right hemisphere grows fastest; then the left begins to overtake. The right hemisphere processes the world non-verbally, through sensations, images and emotions, and looks at the instant 'big picture'. The left hemisphere works more symbolically and verbally, processing things in logical, linear detail. Because the right-brain is more directly connected to the deeper brain, it is less regulated emotionally; it also has a negative bias towards worry, depression and shame, whereas the left-brain is more positive and balanced. So your baby's brain starts with a slight bias towards worry – another reason for showering her with love and care.

Condensed idea
Super-bright brains are formed through satisfying early emotional experiences

17 Taking turns

Babies are very willing to lie back and be entertained, but in time it's important to introduce them to the idea that interaction is a two-way process: your baby's part is just important as anyone else's. And it's not just about playing a part; it's about turn-taking, or give and take.

To and fro

In the first weeks of your baby's life, she's largely passive when it comes to engagement. She won't do much but watch and listen as you talk to her and play with her and comfort her. So it's up to you to encourage her to get involved as soon as she's ready, after about six weeks. She will learn of her own accord, of course, but there are things you can do to 'scaffold' her progress.

There's a 'dialogue' routine so natural that parents often go through it without thinking. When your baby's looking at you with a blank but attentive face, fill in the gap by trying to gently get a response from her by, say, raising your eyebrows, or sticking your tongue out. Wait to see what her response is. If she smiles or gives a flicker of recognition, you can respond in kind. Maybe you could puff your cheeks out and blow gently on her nose, and see if she tries to blow back. (Blowing also helps her to learn breath control and strengthens the muscles used in speech.)

> Chatted about poo to Anna as I changed her nappy. She seemed to find it fascinating! #playfulmum

This might seem just a silly game, but it's actually a rehearsal for the basic skills of adult conversation. When two people talk, they take turns, picking up on subconscious clues when it's time for them to respond. If you doubt that this is a skill, listen to people around you as they talk to one another – how many interrupt another person before they have finished speaking? What are the clues to appropriately 'stepping in'?

You can develop this dialogue with your baby when you play physically responsive games and when you actually talk to her. Engage with her as if she really is responding, encouraging her and giving her time to react to your words. 'How are you doing, sweetie?' (pause...) 'Yes, you are doing well, aren't you?' (pause...). Parents often do this naturally, but it's worth being aware of what's going on and consciously interacting with your baby. When she's a few months old, she may start to fill in those pauses with little reactions. After seven or eight months or so, she may even make little coos, then babble slightly. These are the first steps on the road to talking – even though there's a long way to go.

Give and take

Turn-taking is not just important in conversation; it's a crucial part of all human interaction. And it doesn't come naturally to children; they have to learn it, and it can take a long time. Even when they become toddlers they will still lack the ability to take turns easily, either when playing or when talking. For a long while, they are in a self-centred world of their own, so they haven't learned how to act harmoniously with others.

That's why it's worth taking the trouble to help them in various ways. You can rehearse turn-taking in all kinds of simple communications – when you wave goodbye, blow a kiss or shake your head to say 'No'. You can mimic your baby, too, in whatever she's doing. If she kicks her leg, why not gently kick your leg, too? If she throws a toy on the table, wait until she stops, then pick the toy up and bang on the table too – then give it back to her and let her bang it. And if she throws it down, you throw it too. Make sure she knows it's a game by smiling and remaining relaxed (don't ever start throwing toys angrily!). Think about introducing little changes in response, such as banging the toy on the table twice, to start a dialogue going as she begins to imitate you. You can do the same thing with sounds. If your baby is making a noise with her toy, join in by making the same noise, then take turns. After a while, introduce a little change to the noise and see if she responds.

Turn-taking games

Eventually, as she nears the end of her first year, you'll be able to introduce more structured games, in which turn-taking is part of the rules. When she rolls a car, for instance, pick it up and roll it back to her, and encourage her to roll it to you again. You can do the same with a ball.

Or you can try building things together. You put on one brick, then she puts on another, to build a tower. You could make a giant tower out of old cardboard boxes, after taping them up beforehand to make sure they're nice and rigid. Help her to find the biggest box to put at the

Making your own rituals

Everyday rituals are a great way to encourage turn-taking once your baby gets a little older. Make up a silly little turn-taking ritual to start feeding, for instance, by starting off proceedings by tapping the spoon on the table a couple of times – first you, then your baby – then saying together 'oooh' or 'aaah' (or whatever she can manage). Or when grandma and grandpa come to say goodbye, sing a little rhyme and then kiss her on both cheeks. The humour will help foster the enthusiasm and memory of the game.

bottom as a starting block, and show her what to do. When it gets too tall, lift her up when it's her turn, so she can place her box on top, or let her hold the tower steady at the bottom while you place your box on top, to show how different people in a team can have different roles.

The crucial thing with all these activities is making it absolutely clear to your baby when it is your turn and when it is hers. Always end your turn clearly, and encourage her to start hers. Say, 'Your turn now' or 'My turn now' or whatever seems appropriate. Develop little handover routines to give her clues and time to realize when it's her turn and when it's yours. Gradually, she'll learn just how helpful turn-taking is, and begin to do it of her own accord.

Condensed idea
Learning to take turns paves the way for conversation and building relationships

(18) The resonance circuit

Human brains are very, very different from computers, and in the last two decades scientists have discovered that brain circuitry actually changes and responds as we interact with each other. When baby and parent interact, brain changes occur on both sides.

Mirror neurons

What is remarkable about recent neuroscience discoveries is how they demonstrate that the bonds between us – the feelings that make us human – are right there in our brains. When you look after your baby and he responds to you, your brain circuitry is an active part of the process. Your brain and your baby's brain are what make you engage with each other, and as you interact, the process affects both your brain and his. That's why interaction is so important in those early months; it literally shapes his brain and yours.

About 20 years ago, a team of neuroscientists implanted electrodes in a monkey's brain so they could detect particular neurons that fired in the his brain when, for instance, he ate a nut. Then one scientist picked up a nut and ate it in front of the monkey. To the team's astonishment, the same neurons fired in the monkey's brain as when he had eaten the nut! They had stumbled across a remarkable secret of the brain – mirror neurons. These are nerve cells that fire in the brain when you see someone doing something – just as if you were doing it yourself.

This process doesn't only apply to actions – other people's emotions are also mirrored in our brains. Mirror neurons are probably why yawns are infectious and why laughter spreads. Negative emotions are catching, too, which is why it's so important to be aware of your emotions when you're with your baby. The process is mutual – your brain mirrors what your baby is doing and his brain mirrors you. In this way your baby starts to internally simulate another person's mind, allowing him to empathize with others and guess at their intentions.

Mismatched words and actions

Mirror neurons are incredibly quick; mirrored responses register in people's brains far faster than any verbal message. So any mismatch between what you consciously say or do and how you unconsciously behave towards your baby can cause him confusion and distress. That's why it's important to be aware of just how you're feeling. The positive side is that mirror neurons can foster empathy and attunement between you and your baby. But if you're feeling stressed, you could unconsciously pass this on to your baby through body language or facial expressions, however soothing and calm your words are.

Mirror neurons in the brain mean that your baby is naturally primed to mimic your actions

Little mirrors

Some scientists believe that babies are born with mirror neurons. Experiments that tracked babies' eye movements suggest that newborns have mirror neurons which help them to understand what you're doing when, for instance, you walk across the room. That may in turn help them to walk, too.

However, other scientists believe that babies grow mirror neurons through 'Associated Sequence Learning' (ASL) – where the neurons grow as the baby begins to go through the sequence of movements (such as walking) for himself and finds out what it feels like. If it does work like this, you could encourage mirror neuron growth by helping your baby to copy you as you do things, such as picking up a spoon or throwing a ball. As you take him gently through each step in a sequence, give him plenty of time to think about how it feels to do it. As you repeat the process together, the neurons may gradually develop.

Why you love your baby

What's going on in your brain is just as important as what's going on in your baby's brain. Have you ever wondered why you love your baby? Or why you, like most other parents, are happy to devote so much time and effort looking after your offspring? It transpires that there are circuits in your brain that drive this: circuits engaged in your bond with your baby that operate both on a basic instinctive level and at a higher rational level. If these brain circuits are properly developed, they drive you to look after your baby. And it is likely that the converse is true.

Some neuroscientists call these brain circuits 'resonance circuits' because of the way that your brain and your baby's brain interact as you become attuned to each other. This involves both the mirror neurons and the insula, a tiny part of the brain that links our physical sensations to emotions – turning feelings into conscious thoughts. It connects the physical sensation of hitting your leg to the thought 'I've bumped my leg and it hurts', and allows you to feel the hurt. Together, the

> Freddie seems to know exactly what I'm thinking – his little face wrinkles up whenever I'm thinking hard. #mindreader

mirror neurons and insula are thought to make up a kind of 'imitation and empathy' system. As your baby watches you, and you watch him, your brains run this circuitry, helping you both to work out what might be happening to the other person emotionally. He sees you bump your leg, say 'Ow!' and frown, and he mirrors you internally, 'feeling' your pain. In this way he gets some sense of your emotional state and begins to develop empathy – a sense of how another person feels. In the same way, you watch his face for signs of his emotions and respond to them. The more attuned the two of you become, the more your baby can learn about dealing with emotions and interacting empathically with other people.

What all this reveals is that the way you behave and feel directly influences the way your baby's brain develops. If you want your baby to be happy, you need to work at being happy when he's around. If you want him to be intellectually curious, you must be too. Be the best parent you can be – and you'll help him develop to his fullest potential.

Condensed idea
Your brain and your baby's brain have circuits that respond and develop together

19 Exploring the world

Babies learn about the world through exploration and discovery, and you can help your baby with the wonderfully simple idea of sensory treasure baskets. She will delight and learn as she selects various objects from a basket and touches, tastes and plays with them.

I found it!

The idea behind treasure baskets is an aspect of child development called heuristic play. 'Heuristic' means 'discovery', and it comes from the same root as 'eureka' (meaning 'I found it'). The word was coined by British child psychologist Elinor Goldschmeid in the 1980s to describe the way children learn about objects as they play with them and explore their properties.

> Jamie seems to have fallen in love with a piece of old leather and some orange peel! #treasureseeker

In heuristic play sessions, you present your baby with a basket containing a selection of easy-to-handle natural and found objects (made of any material except plastic) for her to explore using all her senses. The basic idea is nothing new; parents have always known that babies are fascinated by colourful buttons or crinkly wrapping paper, but treasure baskets develop this natural curiosity into a simple teaching tool that works from the time babies can sit unaided.

From birth to the age of around two, babies work hard at trying to make sense of the world, but the only way they can do this is through sensory perceptions and motor activities (physical motions) – hence this developmental stage is known to psychologists as the sensorimotor stage. Essentially, it means that babies explore the world by seeing, feeling, tasting, smelling and listening to objects in the world using the skills they were born with (which include grasping and sucking) and then responding to the sensory stimuli, by smiling or frowning, for example. The heuristic play of the treasure basket provides rich sensory experiences that stimulate development and growth of a baby's brain. The colourful visual experience will usually encourage a baby to reach into the basket to pluck out an object, developing hand-eye coordination. As she grasps and lifts it, she hones her fine motor skills and muscle strength. As she plays, she can focus very deeply, and this is important in helping a baby to develop her own ideas and thought processes.

Discovery time

Treasure baskets are not something you can let a baby loose on by herself. The idea is to set up short, controlled and supervised sessions: 30 minutes to an hour is ideal, three or four times a week, or even every day if your baby is happy. Make sure that for each session, your baby is fed, rested and calm – and take steps to create a very relaxed atmosphere.

Treasure baskets offer a baby lots of opportunities for new sensory experiences

Your presence (or that of another caregiver) is really important if the sessions are to have maximum benefit. Sit nearby and be attentive and responsive, but completely unobtrusive. Your baby needs to know you are there and interested in her exploration, but every choice must be entirely her own and she must be free to make it in her own time. Don't be tempted to 'show' her things or hurry her up, even gently. The basket and its contents are entirely hers.

You'll find yourself fascinated by the way your baby's eye is taken by particular objects and just how she goes about exploring them. The question that your baby is asking herself is: 'What is this object like?'

Themed baskets

One way to ring the changes with your treasure basket is to try themed baskets. Here are some ideas:

- **Food basket:** cleaned fruit and vegetables such as oranges, lemons, bananas, carrots, potatoes, turnips, apples.
- **Nature basket:** pine cones, leaves, large pebbles, shells, dried grass, hemp rope, sheepskin and so on.
- **Textiles basket:** leather, wool (a small knitted square is ideal), tea towel, loofah, nail brush, flannel.
- **Texture basket:** pieces of cloth, ribbon, netting, shiny fabric, towelling, sponge, cardboard tubes.
- **Noisy basket:** anything that makes a sound when she touches it – a bell, a sealed jar filled with dried beans, a bangable tin, wooden objects to tap with.
- **Shiny basket:** old spoon, old CD, bracelet, salt shaker, napkin ring, small mirror.

She'll touch it, grip it, suck it, bang it, stroke it and shake it again and again as she finds out that some objects are rough to the touch, some are smooth, some are light, some are heavy, some make a noise when you shake them or bang them, while others are quiet. Later, when she's a toddler, she will no longer be content with just feeling, mouthing and shaking objects – she'll want to know what she can do with them. Her question then, in heuristic play, will be 'What can I do with this object?' But from 6–12 months, all she wants to do is find out what each object is like.

What goes in your basket?

A treasure basket can be any large, rigid, open container without any sharp edges, but a low, open basket with rigid sides works best, placed on the floor where your baby can easily reach in. Ultimately, you should aim to build up to around 60–80 objects, but you can start with just 10 or so – maybe simple household objects such as an egg box, a pastry brush and a wooden spoon. The collection needs to be continually changed and developed to keep it fresh and interesting; pick up shells when you go to the beach or pine cones when you're in the woods, for instance. Think about different shapes, textures and smells, and include objects that make a noise and those that don't. Once your baby has explored a mixed basket for a while, you could try themed baskets (see box).

Safety is key here, so check that everything is clean and that none of the objects are broken or might be accidentally pulled apart. Avoid objects that are sharp, could easily be swallowed or choked upon, or might contain lead, PVC or imitation leathers (these are toxic to babies).

Condensed idea
Treasure baskets are a cheap, simple and very effective way to stimulate discovery and learning

20 Learning about people

From the age of around 8–10 months, babies begin to read facial expressions and understand how people change their moods. This is an important new stage in your baby's learning about the world and how to respond to it, and it's a significant social development.

Mind-reading babies

By the age of about eight months, your baby will begin to read faces – his parents' in particular. He'll learn that when a person's expression changes, it's because they are feeling differently. Even as a newborn, a baby will copy a parent's expressions, but now your baby is studying faces analytically, trying to work out what's going on. He's trying to read your mind through your facial expressions. Recent research at the

Babies constantly look back towards their carer for reassurance when faced with an object that may or may not be safe

University of Missouri, USA, focusing on 10-month-old babies showed that they could understand what strangers were likely to be thinking, just by looking at their changing expressions.

It's at about this time, too, that your baby will begin to explore the world independently, away from your arms, and that's where his study of facial expressions becomes vital. Whenever he encounters something new – a new toy, place or person – he will look to you for guidance. He'll constantly look back towards your face as he explores, looking for cues in your face as to what's safe and what's not, because this is vital for his survival. This is sometimes referred to as a baby's 'face-check'.

Face-checking

Developmental scientists refer to the way a baby face-checks other people as 'social referencing'. From the age of around 10 months, babies can tell from parents' facial expressions and the tone of their voice what's okay to do and what's not. As adults, we 'social reference' all the time – continually checking others' faces to see if this new person is socially acceptable, or that picture is horrible.

> Baby Ben seems scared of dogs. That's funny – I am too. Uh oh. Is he getting this from me? #cautiousmum

But for babies it's a crucial part of exploring the world safely. As adults, we can choose to ignore social signals, but babies, on the whole, do as they think they've been told – though of course there are exceptions!

A baby's parents are the prime source of his social signals, but he soon begins to take note of all adult faces. In one recent study, a researcher placed two boxes in front of some one-year-old babies. As the researcher looked into the first box, his face took on a look of delight; when he looked into the second, his face showed disgust. When the babies were given the boxes to explore themselves, they only looked in the box that seemed to

Mum or dad?

Research has shown that mums and dads may give different social referencing to their babies:

- In most cultures, mums still tend to perform the majority of childcare, and so they are seen by baby as a 'safe haven'. This means that mum's expression and tone of voice are powerful everyday guides for a baby when questioning the safety of activities or objects.
- Dads, on the other hand, tend to encourage exciting, physical fun and new games. This means that if mum and dad are present, babies often look to dad for guidance in social behaviour. Children of fathers who exhibit socially anxious behaviour are likely to interpret this as a strong negative signal about society in general, and are more likely to become anxious in social situations than children of socially anxious mothers.
- The important thing is for both mum and dad to give the baby the same message; mixed messages are confusing.

have delighted the researcher. They didn't bother to look into the one that produced a look of disgust. Scientists have found that negative reactions have a far stronger effect on babies than positive ones. That's probably because negative signs indicate danger: your baby needs to react instantly to your horrified face if his hand is reaching towards a hot kettle.

Once you know that your baby can pick up on your facial expressions, you can begin to use them to teach him about things in a gentle but deliberate way. You are now his guide to what's safe and what's dangerous, what's right and what's wrong – and even what's funny and what's not. So it's important to be clear and consistent. If he crawls towards a dangling tablecloth, make sure he understands how you feel by jumping up with a clear look of disapproval, and a sharp 'No!' even if there's nothing on the table this time. He might not understand the word 'no' yet, but he'll certainly get the message. Note that if you look unbothered and say 'No' in a mild tone of voice, he might get confused.

You can also use social referencing to introduce your baby to new things, such as new foods and new people. If you're trying to introduce him to some new food, eat a little yourself and say 'Mmm...' and reflect your delight in your facial expression. This will give your baby a signal that the food is safe for him to try. Positive referencing is a much slower form of teaching than the negative version and requires patience, but it's worth persisting. An accidental shudder by you as you eat a new food, for instance, could put baby off that food for a long time.

Are strangers scary?

At about the same age as a baby learns to social reference, he also begins to be frightened of strangers. That's not something to worry about in itself; it reflects how he's learning to rely on you powerfully for guidance, and that's a good thing. Many babies are especially wary of men in hats or dark glasses, because their faces are harder to read. This 'stranger anxiety' isn't easy to overcome, but be patient and gently use positive social referencing to ease your baby's fears by showing how happy and at ease you are with strangers. Obviously it's embarrassing if your baby cries every time grandma walks in the room, but if you can show him that you are happy and relaxed around grandma, you'll slowly win him round.

Condensed idea
By encouraging your baby's ability to read faces, you can help him to feel more confident about exploring his world

(21) Now you see it...

You probably love to play 'peek-a-boo' with your baby and get her gurgling in delight as you suddenly appear from behind your hands to say 'boo!'. In fact, this is more than just a silly game; it has been shown to help babies grasp the key concept of 'object permanence.'

Out of sight, out of mind

Object permanence is basically the idea that objects continue to exist even when you can't see them. Developmental scientists have found out why peek-a-boo is such a delight for babies to play: they think that a person or object ceases to exist when it disappears from view. For babies, objects pop in and out of existence as they impact (or not) on the baby's senses. So if you hide your face behind something like a scarf and then whisk it away so your face reappears, your baby will find this magical. Learning that objects do still exist even when they're out of sight has long been considered to be a crucial stage in a baby's intellectual development. It was thought to happen at around nine months old, but recent research suggests that it may occur as early as four months of age.

You can easily test whether your baby has an understanding of object permanence. Show her a favourite toy and get her interested. Then hide it under a blanket. If she is too young (typically before she's four months old), she'll quickly lose interest – because for her the toy no longer exists; it's 'out of sight, out of mind'. She does not have the intellectual skills yet to imagine or even think about things that she cannot see, feel or hear. If she's not receiving any information about them from her senses, to her they don't exist. After four months or so, if you leave just a part of the toy showing, your baby may begin to realize that the whole toy is still there.

As your baby gets older (between four and eight months), the idea of object permanence will finally begin to dawn, and you'll see her natural curiosity take over as she actively searches beneath the blanket for the disappearing bear or ball, convinced that it still exists. She may still make 'place errors', however, looking for the bear or ball under the blanket where she saw you hiding it yesterday, even though today you showed her that you were hiding it somewhere else, such as behind the chair. This is simply a stage most babies go through as the idea of object permanence begins to settle.

Object permanence: stage testing

Most babies understand object permanence from around 6–8 months old, but you can test their level of development in this area with a simple game:

1 Lay two tea towels or muslins side-by-side on the ground.
2 Encourage your baby's interest in an object (such as a rattle) then let him see you hide it under the left-hand cloth.
3 If your baby finds the object under the cloth, congratulate him. You could pause then, or move to the next step.
4 Take the rattle and let him see you hide it under the left-hand cloth. Then without your baby seeing you do this, move the rattle from the left- to the right-hand cloth. Does your baby look for the rattle under the left-hand cloth (demonstrating that he's grasped the first stage of object permanence)? If so, does he then give up, or does he look under the other cloth? If he continues the search after first being disappointed, he has fully grasped the complete idea of object permanence.

Age and recognition

In the 1920s, Swiss psychologist Jean Piaget argued that the reason object permanence is a key stage of intellectual development is because it allows a baby to realize that the world exists separately from her: she and everything else has a separate existence. He claimed that babies discover the concept in six stages of development. During stage one (0–1 months), babies are too little aware of objects to notice when they vanish from sight. At stage two (1–4 months), they notice objects and follow their movements. At stage three (4–8 months), they are able to find a partially hidden toy (perhaps poking out from under a cushion). Once they reach stage four (8–12 months), babies can find a completely hidden object from where they last saw it (such as behind the sofa). At stage five (12–18 months), they can find an object that has been hidden in their sight, found, then hidden again in a different place. By stage six (18 months plus), babies fully understand the concept of object permanence.

Some developmental scientists today question the ages Piaget suggested for the stages, and have argued that a baby's failure to track hidden objects may have less to do with object permanence than with their

poorly developed working memories. Moreover, Piaget's idea was entirely related to vision, and it may be that sound, smell and touch give a young baby more and different ways of knowing an object's permanence, such as she demonstrates when reaching for you in the dark.

Person permanence

Nonetheless, no one doubts that grasping object permanence is important for a baby, and you can help her along the way by providing a secure and dependable environment for learning and a predictable routine. If there is a sense of permanence and continuity, she will learn and notice much more easily when there are little changes. In the early stages of their lives, babies may not cry when their main caregiver leaves the room. This may be because they are not really aware enough to appreciate that the caregiver has gone. But after eight months or so, just as a baby begins to understand object permanence, she also begins to develop separation anxiety. Once she realizes that mum still exists but has actually gone away, she begins to announce her distress by crying loudly. To lessen

> Uh oh. My baby has now taken to playing 'hide the keys' with me! #Lateforwork

separation anxiety, ease her into it: step just out of sight, then peek in again to let her know you are still near. If you play this disappearing game frequently, gradually leaving just a little bit longer between each reappearance, she'll become generally more relaxed and confident that you'll come back.

Condensed idea
Peek-a-boo helps your baby realize that objects in the world are separate and enduring (even you!)

Memory practice

Scientists used to think that babies couldn't remember much and this explained our lack of very early memories. In fact, babies do remember – they just forget very quickly. However, you can help develop your baby's memory in various ways, with simple, fun routines.

Memory and imitation

Several decades ago, developmental scientists thought that babies couldn't really form memories. That's why, they believed, most of us suffer from 'childhood amnesia' – that is, only very few of us can remember anything at all from our first few years in the world. Scientists believed that young babies did not have the brain architecture to experience the world as anything but a continual blur of messages from the senses. Parents and caregivers felt there might be more going on, but since babies can't tell you what's in their heads, there was no evidence to back up either view.

> I'm convinced my six-month-old can remember things – she gets excited when we turn left out of the door... it's the way to the park. #ducktime

However, scientists have now developed simple tests to detect indirectly what babies do remember. They have found that when 12-month-old babies are shown a 'special way' of playing with a toy, a majority of them can remember how to do it when given the toy again – whether there has been a gap of three minutes or four weeks since the demonstration. It seems that babies learn by watching and copying, and actually pick up on things very well. Brain scans have shown that the neural structures that form memories are pretty much the same in babies' brains as in those of older children and adults. So memories can form even in the brains of newborns; what babies lack is the ability to retrieve the memories, especially in the long-term. If we don't bring memories to mind, they fade away. This may explain childhood amnesia.

Memory boosters

Babies remember things for longer as they get older. A six-month-old baby forgets most things within a few days; he'll remember things for

Surprise bag

A lovely way to aid your baby's memory development when he reaches 10–12 months is to give him a little surprise to look forward to in the morning. Just put a small bag (with a loose opening, not a drawstring) at the foot of his cot last thing at night after he goes to sleep. Pop into it things like a soft animal, his favourite toy, something to make a noise, a picture book, a nest of boxes, and other things he can safely play with on his own. Memory building depends on familiarity – and this idea uses familiarity with a twist. Each time he wakes up, he remembers the excitement of discovery the previous day, and what he found in the bag then. But because the contents are a surprise each morning, it keeps him guessing. This sparks the interest that helps to build memory connections.

up to a month when he's nine months old, and for a few months when he's one year old. He will be two or three years old before he'll be able to retain and recall long-term memories. However, memory retention is initially really variable: some younger babies remember much more than others, but this evens out by the age of around two.

What's crucial in these early memories is repetition. Your baby's memory is quite short-term, so he needs frequent reminders. Also, it helps to create stand-out events that he will recognize as being different in some way. So if you want to encourage him to remember things, aim for lots of stability and repetition, not constant change. That's why daily routines are such a good idea. If you always go through the same ritual of tummy-tickling before his bath, for instance, or sing the same song to him every day when he's being dressed, he'll start to remember an association between being dressed and hearing that song; this enables him to anticipate what's coming and begin to enjoy it. Luckily, a baby won't get bored if you sing the same old nursery rhymes, because to him they're almost new each time. Variety probably means very little when your memory is short! You'll need to be patient, but gradually, through lots of repetition, some rhymes will become familiar. If you want your baby to learn a new skill or find out how to play with a new toy, don't try to introduce it in one long session – he'll get bored, and will have forgotten it by the next day anyway. Instead, show him the skill or the toy briefly for several days in a row, for around five minutes each time. Then top up the memory, if it's important, by showing him the toy every week or so.

Context makes a difference

The chances of your baby remembering something are affected by the circumstances around it. Things are made memorable by attention, emotion and association with different senses. So if you particularly want your baby to remember something, gain his attention by saying his name, then make eye contact by looking directly at him. You'll probably find yourself doing this quite naturally in some circumstances, such as mealtimes, when you might say something like, 'Ben – would you like some apple?'.

Fun and games help, too; babies are much more likely to remember things if they're part of a game or an enjoyable routine. If the activity involves all the senses – especially smell and touch, as well as sight – it's much more memorable. If a friendly dog wanders up, say your baby's name to get his attention and then say 'Dog!' very clearly, as you allow your baby to feel the dog's coat and smell his doggy aroma. Hold his hand out into the rain and say 'Rain!' as his hand feels the raindrops. And every day, at least once, ask if he wants a kiss – then give him one.

Condensed idea
**Babies' memories are short-term,
so the best way to help them develop
is through the repetition of routines**

(23) Baby-talk

If you spoke to an adult the way you speak to your baby ('Whoosa sleepie booboo?') they would think you were mad. But silly baby-talk is your baby's language, and you're actually tapping into a fast-track route to her intellectual development when you use it.

Motherese

It certainly feels natural to talk to babies in a silly, high-pitched, sing-song way, and we all tend to do it without thinking when we interact with them. However, some parents and caregivers are embarrassed to talk this way, and in the past, they would have been reassured by advice that if they wanted their baby to grow up speaking like an adult, they should speak to her like an adult. Recent research has turned this idea on its head: it turns out that baby-talk is good for your baby's development.

One thing that research has confirmed (and any caregiver already knows) is that babies really like listening to baby-talk, sometimes called 'motherese' or, by scientists, 'infant-directed speech'. They tend to switch off with the monotone and long sentences of adult speech, but the modulated excitable sounds of baby-talk and the exaggerated enunciation and the big gestures that go with it grab a baby's attention. This appeal is increased by the fact that baby-talk is a clear sign that the speaker is animated and focused on them.

Baby-talk also seems to have many positive benefits for babies – not least of which is that it helps them develop language skills faster. It's not that they won't learn to speak listening only to adult speech. But babies exposed to baby-talk seem to learn words 25 per cent faster. In fact, some babies only learn words taught to them in baby-talk. Even more significantly, babies of single mums who suffer from depression and can't raise the energy for baby-talk have been found to suffer delayed language development. Fortunately, another parent or caregiver can help to make up for this lack of baby-talk.

> Babbling insanely to baby today in garden. Weird looks from nosy neighbour but kept baby happy! #welovetochatter

The power of baby-talk

Baby-talk works partly because it engages your baby's attention better than more evenly pitched adult speech. This means that she begins to listen carefully, so she is more likely to notice different sounds. Six-month-old babies, for instance, can notice the differences in sound between the syllables of multiple-syllable words if they're spoken in baby-talk. The same words spoken in 'adult talk' go in one ear and out the other! Clear enunciation and exaggerated inflection help a baby to distinguish between words and sentences, while long, drawn-out vowels within words are much easier for her to identify than short ones. What

Speech development in year one

For the first six months, a baby can only cry and coo. But then she will begin to gain enough control over the muscles of her vocal tract to start babbling. Unintelligible though these sounds are, they mark the first steps on the road to speech:

- At six months, a baby can only repeat combinations of consonants and vowels, such baba, booboo, or wawa (this is known as 'reduplicated babbling').
- At 8–9 months, a baby can manage more complex combinations such as da-bak-idi-boo ('variegated babbling').
- At 9–10 months, the babbling will begin to sound a bit like your language, with similar-sounding ups and downs, and syllables ('conversational babbling').

babies hear best in a word is the stressed syllable, which is why a baby's first words are often just repetitions of that: mama, dada, nana, and so on. Surprisingly, it's not just the sounds that baby-talk helps to clarify for your baby; it's the meaning or usage, too. The short sentences, the repetition and the clear phrasing make it easier for her to pick up on words that are repeated, and absorb the structure of language.

Above all, baby-talk probably works because it focuses your mind 100 per cent on your baby, engaging with her and encouraging a response. Studies have shown that when a mother is alone with her baby, she talks about what her little one is doing nearly 70 per cent of the time. This figure is likely to be true of full-time dads too. That degree of attention not only helps strengthen attachment, but also provides baby with a perfect language tutor.

Taking turns to speak

One of the key elements of baby-talk is the attempt to build a conversation, long before a baby can understand a single word of what is said. You might ask your baby, 'Are you ready for din-dins, sweetie?…Are you?…Are you?…', each time waiting for her to respond. Then you might answer yourself by saying something like, 'You are ready, aren't you?' as she seems to wriggle happily. The important thing is that between everything you say, you give her the chance to reply – and imagine what she might say if she could. Eventually she might even give a satisfying look, move or even a gurgle to show she has understood. In this way you might go on having one-way conversations with her all day long.

By using an imaginary dialogue (where you imagine your baby's responses) you are helping her develop a sense of how conversation involves turn-taking. You're also giving her the idea that words can help her say how she is feeling or what she wants. As you wait and try to read her response, you're also fine-tuning your sensitivity to her needs, which is a vital part of building the secure attachment that enables her brain to develop healthily.

Baby-talk conversations can start from the moment a baby is born, but they really take off in the second half of the first year. Your baby won't necessarily understand you, but will enjoy moving and gurgling back as you chatter away. Look for her to respond, and give her plenty of time to do it before you move on – even if it's just a babble, it matters. Imagine how irritated you would feel if your conversation partner interrupted just as you paused momentarily to find the right words!

Condensed idea
Silly-sounding baby-talk is just what your baby needs to develop great communication skills

(24) Learning words

Humans are the only animals that can speak proper languages and adults take many years to learn to speak a foreign language – yet most babies learn to speak in just a few years. It is an astonishing achievement, but babies need all the help they can get.

Beginning to understand words

Imagine how hard it must be for a baby to appreciate what language is. To realize that those sounds have meaning. When a baby emerges into the world, all he hears is people making strange sounds. Initially they're so strange to him that no particular sound is easier to hear than any other, so it all sounds like a continuous 'ratatatat'. Gradually, however, with the help of baby-talk especially, a baby begins to filter out the important sounds and to identify occasional words and phrases that he hears again and again amid the adult murmuring.

> My baby lights up when I say the word 'Scruffy' – the name of my neighbour's dog! #chattymum

However, hearing and distinguishing words is very different from understanding them. It takes a while, for instance, for a baby to realize that words have a meaning – and that particular sounds can be linked to particular things in the real world. Fortunately, human brains are very good at spotting patterns, and eventually he will begin to get the idea. The initial problem is to work out which words mean what. The first words a baby understands are those he hears most often, which is

why most babies start by identifying their own names. A baby may not understand that 'Max' means him, exactly, but he will understand that when he hears the sound of someone saying that, it's worth responding – because it often signals food or fun. You can test this for yourself with your baby: see if he turns to look at you when you call his name.

Other words babies identify early tend to be the names of key people in their lives, such as parents and other family members. These are not easy for a baby to understand, but eventually the day will come when your baby will turn and smile in the right direction when you say, 'Where's daddy?' It's worth helping him with this game, asking him patiently, again and again, where someone is, then directing his gaze with your eyes to the right person.

What's that?

Knowing the names of objects tends to come later, because there are so many things in the world that it's hard for a baby to know what you're talking about when you say, 'That's a cat...C-A-A-A-T'. For all he knows, 'cat' could be the carpet or the table or the cat's fur or its colour or just

Foreign sounds

At six months, babies can still hear the subtle
differences between sounds in all the world's
languages, most of which are inaudible to their
parents. However, between eight and ten months,
they begin to focus on the sounds of their parents'
native language in order to distinguish words – and
so they lose the ability to hear some of the sounds
used in foreign languages. That's why babies exposed to two or
more languages when young are at an advantage when it comes
to learning languages later. The difference between adult and
baby abilities explains the following:

- Japanese babies can hear the difference between 'la' and
  'ra'. Japanese adults cannot.
- European babies can hear the difference between 'p' sounds
  in the Thai language, but European adults can't.
- US babies exposed to Mandarin-speaking for six weeks could
  hear the sounds in Mandarin as well as Taiwanese babies.

about anything else. Movement distinguishes one thing from another –
it makes them stand out as a separate thing from everything else around
them – and studies have shown that babies are more likely to attach
words to things that move, such as people and pets. This is why words
like 'nana' and 'doggy' and 'car-car' are often among the earliest ones
identified and adopted by a baby.

You might think that pointing to an object would help your baby know
what you're talking about. It does in time, but the idea of following a
pointed finger is not an easy one to grasp. Animals never get it. In their

early weeks, babies try to point themselves, beginning with their whole arm and then their hand, before finally isolating a finger. But they're not trying to show you something, they're trying to focus their own attention. When your baby sees you pointing, he will look at your hand rather than in the direction you're pointing. Babies need to be at least six months old before they can begin to follow a pointing finger.

Name everything

For babies under six months' old, it's much better to name things that they are already looking at, or fascinated by, than to point towards something new. When you do want to show your baby something, always wait until he's ready and attentive, then touch or tap the object, pick it up, or even lift him nearer to it, shifting your gaze between him and the object all the time and engaging his attention. Make sure you emphasize clearly the word you want him to hear, putting the word at the end of the sentence. For instance, 'Look, here's a bear, a bear. Isn't it a furry bear?'

While labelling objects seems pretty dull for adults, for babies it's all a fun, intellectually rewarding game. So whenever your baby is in the right mood, take him round the room, show him different things and name them. The more mundane and the more frequently used the better. 'Look, baby, here's a plate. Yes, a plate. It's a yellow plate'. You'll know he's got it if he looks at the plate later when you clearly say the word 'plate'. It doesn't matter at first about the words in between as long as you repeat and stress the name of the object. By the time he is one, he'll begin to pick up phrases rather than just single words.

Condensed idea
Learning that sounds have meaning is a huge leap, and your baby needs all the help you can give him

25 Baby signing

All babies naturally communicate with gestures, even before they can speak. By using sign language with your baby, you can help him express his needs and give him a great head start in learning to speak. Signing also develops thinking skills, by requiring symbolic thought.

Tell me about it

Interest in baby signing began way back in the 19th century, when an American professor noticed that the children of deaf parents developed superior communication abilities. This observation was investigated further by an interpreter for the deaf, Dr Joseph Garcia, who noticed that children of deaf parents communicated with their parents from the age of about six months, using signs, and despite their parents' deafness, went on to have very good language and communication skills.

Babies have demands that they want to communicate from birth, but they lack the means to do so. However, from about the age of seven months, they gain the motor skills necessary for making meaningful hand gestures and these can be used to convey their demands. This means that signing can be used from seven months; around 11 months earlier than a child will learn to speak (typically around 18 months). When your baby can tell you that he's hungry, thirsty or simply wants to play with a particular toy by using a simple sign – such as opening and closing his hand – it significantly reduces the stress for both baby and parent. In this way, signing can go some way to preventing the frustration of a misunderstood baby and reduce tantrums in toddlers. As a baby learns to sign, he is also learning to mirror your movements and make eye contact, giving a boost to the development of social skills.

Talk to the hand

In the 1920s, Russian psychologist Lev Vygotsky recognized that a parent could play a key role in promoting or 'scaffolding' a baby's development, and it seems that sign language might be a key part of the scaffold that helps a child learn to speak. Babies exposed early to sign language have been found to learn to speak earlier, develop a wider vocabulary and have a better understanding of grammar than non-signing babies. The confidence that develops as a result may account for why these babies also seem to be more comfortable than others about asking questions and problem-solving. Signing helps a baby to understand the meaning behind words by linking words to the things it sees; 'cat' is the sound

Where can I learn baby signing?

There are many forms of baby signs, and different ways to learn them. You can make up your own signs – or you can use one of the formal baby sign languages such as American Sign Language or British Sign Language, both of which are widely used in nurseries around the world.

- You can find baby signs in books such as *Baby Signs* by Goodwyn and Acredolo, and *My First Signs* by Child's Play.
- Many towns and cities now offer baby signing classes; check the web for classes near you.
- There are several videos online demonstrating baby signs and when to use them.
- Posters of baby signs are available from some book stores and online, and can act as a useful, handy reminder.

and sign linked to the black furry thing that jumps off the window sill, for instance. In this way it helps a baby make the connection between real objects and abstract symbols. At the same time, it aids a baby's concentration, because when you sign with your baby, he will be looking at your signs and listening to what you're saying; doing both at the same time encourages greater focus. There is growing evidence that signing will help your baby progress faster and more confidently through the stages of cognitive ability – that is, the mental skills involved in learning, remembering, understanding information in terms of abstract symbols and problem solving. As he grows, signing can also help develop his early reading skills, by quickening his understanding when you point to a picture in a book then show the sign for the word.

Signing is especially useful if your baby is coming into a world where he is exposed to several different languages, because it provides a common language that your baby can use everywhere.

Once your baby has learned a few simple signs, you'll find that he can sign when he is hungry, for example, as shown here

Everyday signs

To teach your baby how to sign, simply make the signs yourself when you suspect that your baby is feeling a certain way. For instance, if you think your baby is hungry, look at him and ask, 'Are you hungry?' while making the sign for 'hungry' – raising one hand towards your mouth.

Some of the most useful baby signs are very simple to learn. To sign 'sleepy', rest your hands together under your chin. To ask if his nappy needs changing, hold your belt or trouser top as you ask him. 'Pain' is signed by pointing to your tummy, 'milk' is signed by tapping your hand on your chest, and 'all done' is signed by swinging your hands from side to side. You can sign 'love' too, by crossing your hands over your chest.

> I've been using signs for some of the things that Aki needs every day, like drink, food and bed, and now he signs when he wants them. He's talking to me! #feedmemum

Signing may be useful because it allows parents to introduce new ideas into babies' development in a simple, fun way, extending their mental skills. Some people have claimed that signing promotes the development of neuronal connection in a baby's brain. While we wait for reliable evidence on this front, there is no doubt that signing is fun. Also, your baby will realize that learning new things helps him express himself and communicate with you. However, don't be tempted to replace friendly chatter with signing, because talking to your baby teaches him essential language skills, while also soothing him and making him feel secure.

Condensed idea
Teaching your baby simple signs can reduce frustration and stress for both you and your baby

26 The baby artist

Creativity and art are often associated only with older children, or even adults. But you can nourish the roots of creativity and art in your baby in her very first year. It might seem like play, but it really helps babies to learn that they can reshape their world.

Pollock or Picasso?

Give a baby a tray covered in coloured purée, or a table covered in shaving foam, and she'll dabble in it with huge delight and messiness. She'll spend ages making patterns with her fingers or a spoon, dragging and patting. Her approach is loose to say the least, as she swings her hand this way and that, or even gets both hands stuck in. But who is to say that this spontaneous pattern-making isn't art, even if there's never more than a few squiggles which are gone almost as soon as they are made?

At this age, what matters to a baby most is not what the 'paint' is showing, but the extraordinary sensation of dipping her fingers in it and the sense of control she gets as she changes the pattern on the paper or table. This sense that she can make a mark on the world, can shape and reshape it as she chooses, is an important stage in her intellectual development; she is an independent being who can affect the world around her. Playing like this also offers a valuable grounding for early creativity. Of course, she won't be able to draw anything that is recognizable until she's two or three years old, but gradually, with practice during her second year, her marks will become more controlled and more recognizable as shapes. She may learn to lift her finger from the surface to create separate crosses and lines, and maybe even create geometric shapes like circles and triangles.

Make your own body paint

You can buy special non-toxic body paints
for infants, but they are often quite expensive.
It's easy to make your own:

- You'll need: old, thoroughly clean and dry large baby food jars;
  baby shampoo; powdered tempera paint; spoon and cup.
- Pour some colourless baby shampoo into a jar, until it's around
  one-third full.
- Add the same amount of powdered paint, so the jar is around
  two-thirds full.
- Mix thoroughly with a spoon until it is the consistency of
  porridge. Add more shampoo if it's too thick, or more powdered
  paint if it's too thin.
- Store the paints in a dark cupboard until needed and stir
  thoroughly before using them.
- Rinse off with warm water.

Start early

Parents often delay giving their infants paints and paper until they're
at least two or three years old and able to wield a paintbrush or crayon
properly. But your baby can enjoy and benefit from art activities pretty
much as soon as she can scoot about by herself, at the age of around
nine months. If your baby wants to play with her food, let her. Allow
her to make a mess on the table and revel in manipulating it to and fro.
But give her a safe and cleanable floor, too, or a giant sheet of paper, on
which she can crawl about and make marks to her heart's content. Give
her sauce-textured, non-toxic paints to mess about with (see box above)
and let her experiment with dipping her fingers into the paint, squishing

it, then creating great splodges. Give her bits of paper to tear and fold and dip into the paint. Lay out some fat crayons that she can use to scribble with – if she can – or some stubby brushes, as soon as she can hold them. What your baby creates won't be remotely like art, despite some proud parents' fanciful claims, but she'll love the sensations she's creating, and they will feed her developing brain.

Dabbling fingers and smearing paint is good for large and small muscle development, as well as hand-eye coordination, in younger babies. The later use of crayons, markers and paintbrushes will help your toddler begin to develop the fine motor control she will need in later years for holding a pen and writing.

Your baby will also benefit cognitively as she learns about colours, shapes and the way that mixing colours creates different colours. She'll find out that moving her fingers daubed in paint creates different shapes and patterns depending on her movements and finger pressure. She'll begin to understand the idea

> My friends and I just had a body paint party for our babies. Really fun and very, very messy. Can't wait to do it again! #mrspaintball

of cause and effect – that changing one thing makes another happen. And she will begin to develop her imaginative world and a delight in experimentation – both of which could reap huge dividends in later life, whether she chooses to become a creative artist or a research scientist.

Body painting

Don't be afraid to let your baby thoroughly revel in the paints, providing you have somewhere to wash her and her clothes! Most babies love being let loose to 'paint' wearing nothing but a nappy, so if you want to do this, make sure the room is really warm, cover the floor in paper or polythene, then take off all or most of her clothes, and give her cuploads

of paint to play with. On a warm day, you can do it outside and hose everything down afterwards (give her a warm bath, though!). Let your baby paint her body, roll in it, squish it through her hair – even try it for taste – but make sure she doesn't mistake it for a meal and eat vast quantities.

Body painting is huge fun for a baby – and if you can get a few babies together to body paint together, so much the better. Most babies at this age will play by themselves, but when each body is a canvas, they often begin to play together, and it's a great way to reach the beginnings of social interaction. Of course, there'll be a big mess to clean up afterwards, but ask your baby to help do whatever she can to clean up with you. That's as much a part of the activity as the paint splurge; turn this into a fun routine and she'll enjoy it just as much, with obvious benefits later on!

Condensed idea
Babies learn that they can impact on the world by playing with paints at an early age

27 Social baby

Human beings are social animals and our intellectual development depends on interaction with other people. While your baby's relationship with his parents will always be the most important, his mental and social development benefit from spending time with others.

Looking at you

For the first few months after birth, the only interaction that a baby is interested in is with his primary caregivers – normally mum and dad. But gradually he'll begin to look beyond them and notice other people. At around four months, your baby may begin to smile and gurgle at new faces that come into his life, even though he reserves his deepest enthusiasm for his parents. Babies are fascinated by faces and expect a response; research has shown that if a moving object stops moving, it causes a baby to lose interest, but if a person's face becomes still for some time, the baby tries to create a response, through touch and sound.

At about seven months of age, babies begin to look around themselves more extensively and may even become fleetingly interested in other babies (they may briefly coo and mimic each other's sounds, but mostly they remain preoccupied with their own activities). However, while babies of this age are happy to watch other babies, children and perhaps adults, their newfound interaction with the world seems to make them become aware of its dangers for the first time. They begin to become much more nervous of unfamiliar people – and 'unfamiliar people' may include someone he knows, such as an aunt he hasn't seen for a few weeks. You may find that your baby will cry just looking at strangers, let alone being touched or handed to them.

Don't leave me!

This 'stranger anxiety' is very common in babies between seven and 18 months. Although it can cause distress and embarrassment, especially if your baby cries loudly when your sister tries to hold him, it is usually nothing to worry about. You simply need to give him time to adjust at his own pace. Introduce him to new people (or people he's forgotten!) gently and reassuringly. If your baby does get upset when grandma or the new babysitter tries to hold him, don't think

that you need to be firm and push him onto them anyway. It's far better to let him come back into the comfort of your arms so that he can get to know the 'stranger' gradually from that position of safety. Pushing him simply makes him nervous of the unknown, not more resilient towards it. While he's safe in your arms, he might be happy to gently interact with the stranger. Work on getting him completely comfortable in your arms while the stranger plays and talks to him. Only when you feel he's completely ready, let the stranger try taking him again, making sure he can see you smiling and nodding to show that the stranger is safe. Stay close by for a while, then gradually move away – always be ready to come back if your baby seems upset. If there are likely to be long periods of time between visits, keep the memory of the person fresh by showing your baby photos of them.

Tellingly, this is also the time when a baby may also become prone to 'separation anxiety', which means that he becomes anxious at the moment of parting from his primary caregiver. By this time, your baby's mind is developed enough to realize how important you are to him, and his memory is developed enough to notice when you're gone for any time. So don't be surprised if your baby suddenly becomes very anxious when you leave him, even in the company of someone familiar. Always allow enough time for a gentle handover period.

Sociable games for babies

Some games, such as clapping and dancing games, can encourage babies to engage in group activities and help them learn new social interaction tools, from hand movements (such as shaking hands or clapping) to new facial expressions. Most babies learn to clap their hands at 9–12 months, and clapping games are even more fun for a baby if they're played with others about the same age. Clapping is also great for developing muscles, hand-eye coordination and learning about rhythm, so it's a good place to start.

Your baby may need help with clapping at first, so be patient, encourage signs of him mimicking you, and relax in the knowledge that he'll eventually get the hang of it. Learning to recognize and anticipate movements and words will increase his confidence:

- Try clapping along to the rhythm of nursery rhymes such as 'Pat-a-cake', 'Three Blind Mice' and 'Humpty Dumpty'. Help your baby to clap if he enjoys it.
- Try songs, too, such as 'If You're Happy and You Know It' and 'Old MacDonald Had a Farm'. Even if your baby is too young to join in, he'll take pleasure in watching you and the other parents and children.

Making friends

It's important not to let your baby's new-found fears get in the way of social contact. All babies are different; like adults, some babies are sociable and some are not, but all of them need to be introduced to the world of other people. Being around others will enrich his experience of human life, giving him the opportunity to take part in a range of situations that you alone can't provide.

By the end of their first year, most babies revel in the company of their immediate family and enjoy being the centre of attention. Once your baby can move around on his own (from around eight months onwards) you could introduce him gradually to babies of his own age. The best way is by meeting friends with babies in a public place such as a park, where he feels relaxed and there are plenty of people around. Don't expect instant companionship. There's a high chance the babies will take little interest in each other, since babies of this age are usually either preoccupied by their own games (in what experts call 'parallel play') or happy just to watch the other child. Babies don't share or take turns readily at this age. They may form friendships, but it takes time, and you shouldn't be surprised or worried if your baby remains wary of others for some time to come.

> Thought I'd go for a jog while baby was with gran, but underestimated the trauma! Now out jogging with baby in pushchair. #fittermum

Condensed idea
Helping your baby interact with other people will help him learn new social skills and ease the feeling of 'stranger danger'

(28) Mind games

As your baby's memory and sense of independent existence improve towards the end of her first year, she will be able to play in an entirely different way. You can help her play much more interesting games that will really help her mental development.

Growing links

What is most marked about the age of around 10 months is that a baby is clearly aware of the independent existence of objects – she can tell that they are not part of her. In her visual field, she can make out what is part of a book, for instance, and what is part of the table it's lying on. She can also begin to make plans and follow them through without forgetting what she's trying to do before she completes them. She can hold pictures of different things in her head and make simple links. All this will begin to show in the way that she begins to handle toys differently, understanding that each has a different quality and can be played with in particular ways – not simply touched and tasted. She'll cuddle a soft toy in the same ways she feels and sees you cuddling her. She'll also begin to imagine that her doll has a life like her own. If you give her a new toy to hold at this age, she won't simply grab it or pull it to her mouth; she'll think for a while and try to work out what can be done with it.

Hiding games

To make the most of these new developments, you can offer her toys and games that will stretch her and motivate her to think more about the world and how it operates. Hide-and-seek is a great game, because it

Tidying up is fun

One great way to help your baby learn categorization, while also teaching her the value of helping another human being, is to enlist her help at clean-up times. For you it may be a chore, but for her it can just be an extension of the game. Encourage her to say 'Night-night!' to each toy as she puts it away in a box or cupboard. As she learns that stuffed animals go in one place, cars and wheeled toys in another, and bricks in a third, your baby will learn that objects can be grouped and classified. By doing this on a regular basis, she will also begin to think about looking after things.

provides the same delight your baby got from peek-a-boo when she was younger, but takes it to a new level, in which she knows what's going on and can play a far more active role. You can play it with her by yourself, but it's much better if you involve the whole family or friends she is familiar with. It makes it much more exciting if she can hide too, as well as seek. This encourages her to imagine where she might hide herself. If you ask someone to supervise (generally keep an eye on the baby and her environment) while the rest of you play, the hiding and seeking will seem more real. Even mum or dad is hiding! Where are they? Your inclusion makes it more exciting for her and spurs her to think how she might escape detection when she is hiding – which means imagining things from the seeker's point of view. This is a big conceptual step for a baby. And of course, many babies love it if it all develops into a chase!

Obstacle courses are great fun, too. Find some big cushions (blocky sofa-seat cushions work well) or some very stable chairs, then put them in lines and drape them with fabric so they form tunnels and caves for your

baby to crawl through. You can make even more elaborate tunnels and caves, and little nests, out of cardboard boxes. If you want the game to last longer, distribute fun things for her to find as she moves around, so she gains a sense of discovery through adventure.

You can also use an obstacle course of cushions and cardboard boxes to form a challenge that your baby has to surmount to reach you or a favourite toy, for instance. Having to plan and picture how to reach her goal will stretch her thinking in an enjoyable way. Don't make it too hard for her, and always intervene if she looks distressed or worried at any point. You may find that after playing this for a while, she will become confident enough to go exploring by herself without a target. Games like these help develop motor skills and hand-eye coordination as well as cognitive skills, such as planning.

Where is it?

Hiding games are equally valuable. Hide a favourite toy among other objects on the floor and see if your baby can locate it. Ask her where it is, using your voice, facial expression and hands. Give her plenty of time, and shower her with praise if she succeeds. As an alternative game, hide the toy under three towels. Show her where you're hiding it and see if she can find it. Leave part of the toy showing if she's having trouble at first. A nice variation on this is to put a little toy inside a cardboard tube so that she has to tip the tube to get it out. Lifting tubes, towels and cushions is all good practice for motor skills, besides the cognitive stimulus the hunt gives her.

You can take this hunting game a step further with a lucky-dip. Fill a plastic bucket or a cardboard box with screwed up bits of paper and put it in front of your baby. Let her watch as you hide a favourite toy amongst the paper, then let her scrabble around to find it. When she's a little older, you might try the same with a bowl full of dried pasta or rice, perhaps hiding something (or things) that are quite small and tricky for little fingers to handle.

My 11-month-old loves throwing games – especially throw the wet sponge at Daddy. #Humantarget

Hiding games don't always have to be visual. Why not try hiding a loudly ticking clock or a musical box under a cushion or a towel for her to find? This is not an easy game, so help her all you can to start with. Put your hand to your ear, and ask 'What's that?'. This game is a real boost for your baby's auditory development, because she has to hear and identify particular sounds, and also work out where they're coming from. Sound direction is a really valuable skill for a child to acquire.

Condensed idea
You can help your baby make the step to far more complex play towards the end of her first year

(29) Stories and books

Reading gently out loud to your baby and telling stories to him are two of the best things you can do for him. There are few better activities for establishing a bond between you, and if they help create an early love of books, it's something that will benefit him all his life.

Read to me

The value of reading out loud to your baby and storytelling generally has been proven by a good deal of research. These activities gently lead your baby into the vivid and stimulating world of books and help him positively associate them with warmth and comfort. Your reading out loud to him foreshadows the reading process, giving him a feel for how books are structured and how books create an imaginary world, preparing him for the time when he will start to read himself.

Reading will fire your baby's imagination, too. Once he begins to understand what you are reading, it will open up his mind to a range of experiences beyond the everyday; and if you show him pictures, he may begin to see that pictures can represent real things. He may start to create pictures in his head, which is a key part of his mental development at this stage. And of course it's a very effective and entrancing way of teaching him all sorts of things without it ever feeling like a lesson.

> My one-year-old now claps every time we hear about monkey's triumph at the end of the story. How does he know? #storydad

Even before your baby can understand anything you read or tell in a story, he'll benefit from the calming effect of storytelling and the way it strengthens the bond between you. That's why reading can start at almost any age. Your baby is never too young to enjoy a story. In the first few months, of course, he won't understand a word you say, but he'll love being close to you, held snugly in your lap and being bathed in the gentle murmur of your voice with its ups and downs. That's why rhythmic stories, with rhymes and a steady beat, are so perfect for younger babies.

Reading together

As your baby gets a little older, you can involve him in the reading process more and more. Long before he actually understands the words, you can show him what you're doing, and encourage him to turn the pages and look at the pictures. You can even identify words and pictures on the page so that he slowly gets the idea of what you're doing.

Books babies love

There are some books that seem to be loved by children around the world and which don't lose their appeal no matter how many times they are read or heard. The following books fall into this category.

- *The Very Hungry Caterpillar* by Eric Carle. Small fingers love the hole that runs through the book, through which the caterpillar crawls on his voracious journey to becoming a butterfly.
- *The Baby's Catalogue* by Janet and Allan Ahlberg. This book does not have a story but is full of pictures of objects that are very familiar to babies, so is good for teaching them the names of things.
- *Moo, Baa, La la la* by Sandra Boynton. A really fun book full of pictures of animals that will make you smile and give you plenty of scope for making all kinds of silly animal noises.
- *We're Going on a Bear Hunt* by Michael Rosen, illustrated by Helen Oxenbury. Older babies will love the onomatopoeic words and the lovely rhythmic language – great for reading out loud together and learning off by heart.
- *Dear Zoo* by Rod Campbell. Here the storyteller writes to the zoo asking them to send him a pet. Each recommendation is revealed under a tempting flap. Ask baby which animal he thinks is coming next.
- *Dr Seuss's Sleep Book*. This is really for two-year-olds (who just can't go to sleep) but you can have fun with the sounds and the wonderful yawning creatures even when your baby is much younger.

Even if your baby stares blankly at the page, carry on pointing things out to him as if he has taken notice. Make it a shared activity. It may require a little patience and gentle encouragement over quite a long time – just like those imaginary conversations you have with him in which you leave space for his imagined response (see page 95). But eventually he'll get the message and respond. There's no need to push him, but quiet persistence should pay off in the long run. Try to get into the habit of reading or telling a story for at least 20 minutes on most days. Don't try to do it when your baby is agitated, fidgety or too tired. Ideally, find time just before it's time for him to go to sleep, but while he's still alert.

Books for babies

All kinds of books are now on the market for under-twos, many made of fabric and board, which will provide your baby with the experience of exciting colours, shapes and textures as well as the sounds of the words. Some have flaps to lift and tails to pull. You don't need a lot of books when he's this young, and might want to save money now so you can buy more later on, when he's older and does need variety. At this age, your baby can learn just as much from exploring the same few stories again and again as from hearing new ones. In fact the very familiarity will help his memory skills; read with lots of expression and you'll soon find he begins to remember and anticipate what kind of thing happens next. Also, your stories don't have to come from books. If you're feeling in the mood, why not make up your own? Simply tell him things that have happened in your life, from what you did at the shops today to how you met mummy or daddy. Watch his face and if he looks tired, you can always turn the story into a musical and sing a lullaby!

Condensed idea
Storytelling helps children develop language and memory skills, and fires up the inner world of imagination

30 I see, you see

By the time he is one year old, your baby will begin to have some sense that you and he are separate individuals, and it will be quite a challenge for him to work out what this means. Your effort to understand things from his point of view will really help him.

The beginnings of communication

Deep down most of us are convinced of our own importance, even as adults. But every baby truly thinks of himself as the centre of the world and sees everything revolve around him. It seems to him as if things only have their existence because he sees them. Things seem to happen at first because he makes them so. But gradually, as he nears the end of his first year, he starts to see the limits of his power.

He begins to see that when he wants his teddy bear, it doesn't just come to him from across the floor. By himself, he doesn't have the magic powers needed to bring the bear closer, but he starts to learn that you can help him – he doesn't have to do things alone. However, to get your help, he needs to communicate. It's the discovery that he cannot control the world and that he needs help from others that is the spur to communication.

Even once we can speak fluently, we are often misunderstood or misunderstand – and it is deeply frustrating. Think how much more so it must be for a baby who depends so entirely on you for all his needs – and does not even have words to communicate. That's why it will matter so much to him that you try to understand those signals and gestures he uses to tell you what he's feeling. At the same time, it is equally valuable for him to start to learn that you, too, have feelings and wishes separate from his, which you wish to communicate through various signals and gestures. This process of separation can be alarming for some parents and exhilarating for others, but either way, be assured that it is an essential part of your baby's psychological development.

Exciting anticipation

You can encourage the growth of mutual understanding through anticipation games that seem so simple and natural that it's hard to believe that they are genuinely valuable. You may already have played an anticipation game – where you bounce your baby on your knee and then pause for a moment before shooting him up in the air, then both collapsing in giggles. It's the pause and anticipation that matters. Each

Act as though you're his puppet

A baby believes that the world revolves around him – this is how he experiences it. Sitting at the centre of the world, he feels very, very clever when he makes things happen. It's worth playing little games that make the most of this infant delight, because it gives him an incentive to communicate. You could try developing a response to little gestures and sounds that he makes, to entertain him. For example:

- When your baby bangs his spoon on the table, shake your head in the same rhythm and make a silly noise.
- When he gurgles in a certain way, make teddy dance.
- When he nods his head, sing him a little song.

time you sit still and look at your baby between bounces, then wink, he's hooked. When are you going to throw him in the air again? He will hang on your every little movement and expression, trying to guess just when you're going for the bounce. And it's in that pause – a moment of keen engagement – that communication and understanding begin to develop. He begins to look for clues to your intentions – and you, to play the game, should also look to him, to find the right moment to give him the maximum pleasure of surprise.

It's the same with simple games such as 'Round and round the garden, like a teddy bear', where you tap two fingers on the palm of his hand to build up excitement while saying the lines, before doing a sudden two-finger dash up his arm to tickle him, saying: 'One step, two step, tickly under there!' The crucial things are the pause and the interplay, so make the most of these and enjoy them to the maximum. It might seem like the ultimate in silly games. But for babies, games are lessons; the more fun the better – and that goes for you, too.

Looking for cues

However enthusiastic you both are, it's never a good idea to push your baby to play games when he doesn't want to. There are times when he will want to play these games and times when he won't, or he may be happy to play for a couple of minutes but no longer. Picking up on the clues he gives you is also an important part of his growth in understanding: he'll realize that you pick up on his needs – and this means that you understand him and that his needs matter to you.

> Just realized that whenever Tom has had enough of a game he stares out the window. I'm a slow learner! #nomorethanks

What's your baby saying?

Your baby's behaviour has meaning, whatever he's doing. Every baby has his own ways of communicating, so your task is to work out what your baby means when he does certain things. Take the time to observe him and work out what he's feeling or looking for. Listen to the sounds he makes. Does he sound happy or bored? Look at the expression on his face. Where is he gazing? If he looks away, it might be that he's had enough. If you can't understand a particular behaviour, don't worry. It doesn't matter if you thought he was asking for the toy car when he gestures loosely at the bit of fluff on the floor that intrigues him. It's the willingness to try to understand that counts.

Condensed idea
Learning to understand your baby and helping him to understand you is the start of real communication

31 Nursery time

For some parents, sending a baby to a day care nursery is a real wrench – a depressing necessity forced on them by financial or family circumstances. If this applies to you, you'll be glad to hear that some psychologists think the nursery experience may actually be beneficial.

Day care worries

In 1986, American psychologist Jay Belsky published research showing that babies looked after in day care were more aggressive and disobedient later in life. Ever since, there has been a fierce debate about whether day care is right for babies under two. Emotions run high because there's so much at stake: some people argue that day care is damaging to children, while others argue that it provides good care for babies and those that say otherwise are nostalgic and seek to tie mothers to the kitchen sink.

The research is indeed inconclusive and conflicting. A Dutch study in 2006, for instance, found that infants in day care showed moderately raised levels of cortisol, the stress hormone, and other research showed that day care babies are very slightly more aggressive when they go to school. Other research, however, seems to indicate that the effect is mild or diminishes as the child gets older – and many argue that a little more self-assertion is not a bad thing. Further research has shown that day care can have a

> Don't know why I worried about sending Jacob to nursery, he was up at five this morning wanting to go back NOW!! #Iwanttogotoo

positive effect on cognitive and language development, and can help children form better relationships when they go to school. Meanwhile, the number of babies put into day care has risen steadily. In the UK, 277,000 under-threes attend nurseries; in the USA, more than half of all children go to nursery. These figures reflect the need or desire of women to work; in some ways, the argument over whether day care is ultimately a beneficial or harmful thing has been overtaken by social norms and economic necessity.

The jury is out, so parents need to make a decision based on their particular circumstances. It seems that the most critical thing is the type of care on offer, whether at home or in a nursery; what children really need is responsive care in a welcoming environment. In addition, there is every reason to believe that if your baby is properly supported at home, she will reap the benefits of day care rather than suffer from any negative effects.

Personal choice

There is tremendous variation in the quality of childcare on offer, so it's worth putting as much time as you can afford into finding the right place. Do your research on the internet, ask around among friends and neighbours, but above all, visit potential places for yourself. Every baby is different and will thrive in different places, and you are the best judge, by far, of which place is best for her. It might be that she is happiest in a big place with lots of fun facilities, or in a smaller setting which seems more personal. Only you can really say.

What do children do at nursery?

Here are some of the activities you should expect to find on offer within a nursery. Ask the staff how they handle each of these and why they are important:

- **Messy play:** to encourage motor skills, coordination and creativity.
- **Water and sand play:** to help children understand volume, turn-taking and problem solving.
- **Sensory baskets:** to encourage motor skills (fine and gross), knowledge of objects and sensory development.
- **Music, singing and nursery rhymes:** to help develop memory, sound recognition, communication and motor skills.
- **Bricks, boxes and shapes:** this type of play helps children with problem solving, number skills, sequencing and ordering.
- **Dressing up:** a fun way to encourage imaginative play and thinking.
- **Story time:** this aids memory, literacy and language, and communication skills.
- **Outdoor play:** this helps to develop gross motor skills, coordination and social skills, and gives your child an experience of nature.

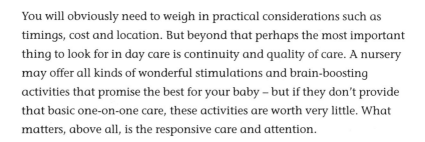

You will obviously need to weigh in practical considerations such as timings, cost and location. But beyond that perhaps the most important thing to look for in day care is continuity and quality of care. A nursery may offer all kinds of wonderful stimulations and brain-boosting activities that promise the best for your baby – but if they don't provide that basic one-on-one care, these activities are worth very little. What matters, above all, is the responsive care and attention.

One-on-one

It is hugely important for babies under two to develop strong attachments, because this is how they learn to manage their feelings (see pages 24–27), but the quick turnover of relationships in some nurseries can make this impossible. Nursery managers are in the business of selling their setting, so when you visit a nursery, ask to visit the room where your baby will spend the day and meet the carers who'll look after her directly. Arrange to see the nursery on a normal day, rather than an open day, to see how the nursery and carers operate on an everyday basis. Look particularly at how the staff and babies interact with each other.

Find out as much as you can about how the carers look after their charges and how long carers stay, on average. Some nurseries leave much of the care in the hands of young, inexperienced or poorly qualified staff – it's worth asking what qualifications the carers do have. A day care centre that has a rapid turnover of staff is unlikely to provide the kind of stability and strong attachments your baby needs. Of course, staff do need to move on every now and then – so ask how the centre handles these transitions. Try to judge for yourself whether each baby is getting proper attention from the carers. Ask how many babies each carer has to look after on a day-to-day basis and what happens when staff are absent. If you can, take your little one in for a brief trial session and see how she responds to the setting and how the carers respond to her. Of course, a bad response isn't necessarily conclusive – since your baby may find even the perfect place takes a little getting used to – but you may get a feeling of whether it's right from how the carers respond to her worries and your own.

Condensed idea
Sending your baby to a day care nursery can be very positive, if you find a place that feels exactly right for your child

(32) Good natured

Once your baby can crawl or toddle, try to take him outside on regular nature walks. Whether you live in the midst of a city or out in the untamed wilds, there is plenty for your baby to gain from the experience of being in the outdoor world.

Denatured

Most of us think that the natural world is a wonderful thing, and many of our most precious childhood memories may be linked to the big outdoors in some way. So it's not surprising that we want our children to grow up with a love of nature. But it may actually be more crucial than that. In 2005, American author Richard Louv coined the phrase 'nature deficit disorder' (NDD) to describe the adverse effect on children of the modern, largely indoor lifestyle. In the UK, two-thirds of children

play outside less than once a week, and one in three have never been on a country walk. Although it's not yet a recognized medical condition, Louv contends that nature deficit disorder leads to 'diminished use of the senses, attention difficulties and higher rates of physical and emotional illnesses'. Some experts even link it to the rise in obesity.

Most of these worries, are, of course, about older children, but there is every reason to believe that the earlier you help young ones get out and experience nature, the more they'll be used to it being a part of their lives. There are the obvious health benefits of sunshine and fresh air, as well as the educational benefits of learning about nature and related science. In addition, nature walks – especially with occasional pauses for exploratory crawling – will help your baby develop his motor skills, as he learns to move over varied and uneven surfaces and tries to touch and grip different things. Nature provides a rich range of sensory experiences, far beyond what you can provide at home, from the smell of damp earth to the texture of bark and dry leaves.

> We went to the woods the other day and Josie spent ages just kicking through the leaves. She loved it! #backtonature

Getting outdoors

A nature walk doesn't have to be a hike in the woods or even the park; quiet pavements lined with hedges and trees or your own back garden are quite enough. in the garden, spread a blanket on the ground and let your baby play with the grass or feel twigs. Look for fascinating insects and other signs of life nearby. When you plant seeds or flowers, let your baby help, and explain what you're doing as you do it. Let him help you water the seeds using a small can, and explain why the flowers need it. You might want to give him his own little patch of flowers (see page 13 for ideas), or plant some vegetables to eat later in the year.

Themed walks

There are all kinds of things you can do with toddlers to encourage their curiosity and love of nature. Here are some ideas:

- Make a collection of different leaves. See if your child can identify the different shapes and colours.
- Study minibeasts through a magnifying glass and, if you know they are safe, encourage him to let the insects crawl over him.
- Collect small rocks and stones to build a home collection.
- Look for and compare different colours in nature, especially the greens, browns and yellows.
- Look for different textures within a natural environment. What things are hard, what soft, what smooth, what crumbly?
- What can you smell? Grass? Flowers? Earth? Farm animals?

When the two of you walk to the local shop, take time to pause and look at the weeds growing in cracks, the lichen clinging to walls and the flowers in window-boxes. Children often stop to wonder about puddles, but their parents usually tell them to 'Come on!'. Instead, take time to pause with your child. Listen to the birds amid the traffic noise. Look at the clouds and the greenery around you. Encourage your child to look, touch and smell the extraordinary world all around you.

Nature walk

If you can, take your child on a 'proper' nature walk to the local park or woods, where he can see and experience nature in abundance. Make sure he's dressed in clothes that will keep him warm and that you're happy to see completely mucky (a packet of wet wipes is always a useful extra). You can just walk out with no preparation and encourage him to look by asking questions. What plants can you see? How big do you think it will grow? Can you see a tree? Is that an ant? And so on. If you don't see any animals, look for signs that they have been there. Just be patient, walk slowly and stop continually to let him explore for himself. Introduce new words by naming things, such as 'leaves' or 'bark'.

Even better, take a little basic equipment to help you both explore nature more closely. A magnifying glass is wonderful for studying minibeasts such as beetles. Take some sheets of white paper with you, to scatter minibeasts and leaves on there and then, so your baby can see them clearly. Perhaps even a few glass jars, to contain insects while he studies them closely and at length, or to take home. A simple camera is great for taking snaps of the different things you both see, so that you can print them out or show them onscreen later, and talk about them. Try to get your child really involved, picking things up for himself – feeling, touching, smelling, listening – and collecting small objects such as leaves, sticks, stones and pine cones to take home. Take a small plastic bucket that he can carry and use for collecting things, and a backpack and containers for you to carry home larger, heavier things for him.

When you get home, help your child to make a nature scrapbook, by sticking in the items that he found (don't worry if this is quite messy!). You can make a simple flower press by putting a cutting (such as a leaf or flower) between two sheets of newspaper, placing this inside a heavy book such as a telephone directory, then placing a heavy object on top. The dried cutting will be ready for the scrapbook just three days later.

Condensed idea
Regular outdoor walks will teach your child about nature and it's great for sensory and motor development

33 Sensory play

It's easy to assume that the best way to stimulate your growing baby's developing brain is to give her mind-based activities. In fact, it's equally important to aid her continuing sensory development, so give her lots of opportunities to explore the world using all her senses.

Engaging with the world

The wonderful thing about sensory play is that older babies and toddlers love it. They are out-and-out sensualists. You only have to see toddlers stomping in puddles, smearing their food all over the table, or banging their spoons in sheer delight to know that they revel in each and every sensory experience. As we get older we forget about the pleasure such simple things can give. However, you can be sure that if your toddler is enjoying something that much – even if she is making a huge mess – she is thoroughly engaged. This engagement signifies that there is plenty of activity going on in her brain, and brain activity promotes development. Some research has suggested that toddlers who are exposed to a wide range of sensory experiences benefit later in terms of IQ scores. For a child, sensory play is an opportunity to explore, experiment, manipulate and observe. It's a chance to discover the world around her, and may mark the beginnings of an absorption that ultimately turns into a successful artistic or scientific career.

The idea of sensory play is to give your toddler a range of sensory materials that encourage her to touch, see, taste, smell and hear. The crucial thing is hands-on experience – and that she is free to undertake this exploratory play in her own way. Besides the obvious benefits to the senses, sensory play helps in many other forms of development, including refining motor skills as she manipulates things, creativity as she plays with a rich range of materials, and cognitive development as she observes and experiments.

Making a mess

Sensory play is really about exploration. But it is frequently very messy, so it's great to set up a space where your child can be as messy as she likes without you worrying about the carpet or the decor. If you don't have a suitable room, get a large, tough plastic sheet that she can splash about on to her heart's content. Failing that, the bathtub might do! All you need by way of equipment is an arrangement of trays or plastic bowls, filled with either sand or water that your toddler can dig in to, splash around and slop about. There are no instructions – just let her loose. Besides sand and water, you can try all kinds of other materials that feel different; consider all the gooey, gloopy, slimy, mushy materials that toddlers love. Shaving foam, jelly, cooked pasta, dry pasta, cooked and uncooked rice, leaves, ice cubes, dry peas and beans, sawdust, sea shells and shredded paper will all do. They don't have to be in pristine

Make your own goo!

There are all kinds of sensory play materials you can mix up at home for a toddler to start experimenting with. Here are a few ideas:

- **Fingerpaints**: mix bright drops of food colouring into plain yogurt. Let your toddler paint it onto a table or tray with her finger. When she's finished, lay a piece of paper over her painting to take a print to keep.
- **Oobleck**: mix one part water to two parts cornflour or custard powder, with a couple of drops of green food colouring. Stir for around 10 minutes to form one perfect blobby thing that echoes the qualities of the green 'oobleck' in the Dr Seuss book, *Bartholomew and the Oobleck*. It's usually liquid, but when you press on it, it magically goes solid. This messy fun is even better if you've read the Dr Seuss book together.
- **Edible silly putty**: mix together 0.5 kg (2 cups) peanut butter; 6 tbsp honey; around 50 g (¾ cup) skimmed, dried milk and cocoa powder. Add just enough dried milk to make the dough pliable. Shape and decorate with edible treats. Eat only in small quantities!

condition. A toddler won't normally care if they're mixed up a bit (though some might demand organization!), so don't feel you have to start with just one new material each time. Choose only things that won't degrade or disintegrate over time, and watch carefully to make sure she doesn't eat food and non-food items. (Also look out for signs of allergies.) To increase the fun, start a collection of tools that she can use to help her explore the sensory materials. Spoons, cups, funnels, scoops, jars, tongs, sponges, cloths, eyedroppers, cardboards rolls and bowls are all useful. In fact, you can select pretty much anything you feel you can safely give her.

Five senses

You can also target activities on one of the major senses. If you want to focus on her hearing development, for instance, you could try filling plastic tubs with various different materials (such as paper clips, coins, rice, buttons or peas) to make a rattle. Then give them to her to shake and encourage her to notice the differences. For smell, put cottonwool soaked in something scented (such as orange juice or chocolate sauce) into separate tubs, turn them over and make a little hole on the tub bottom (now at the top) for her to sniff into. For sight, try putting three or four objects on a tray, move it away,

> Toddler having thrilling time, so I'm ignoring the mess for as long as poss. Hope no one visits! #creativemum

then replace one of the objects and see if she notices any difference. For taste, put tiny quantities of various baby foods in separate bowls. See if she can identify – and has a preference for – any of them. For touch, hide various toys inside a bowl of raw oatmeal and let her dig them out. Or make a texture and colour book for her to flick through, featuring things that look and feel different to one another. As she goes through the book, tell her a little about each of the entries and ask what she notices about them. Be prepared for some surprising responses!

Condensed idea
Sensory play is a central part of a toddler's development, so give her senses a regular workout

(34) Learning environment

A toddler won't learn everything he needs to know from his parents, because he is awake and looking around him for many more hours than he gets direct attention. He can learn a huge amount just from his surroundings, which constantly change.

Exciting surroundings

All of us are powerfully influenced by our environment. Think how much easier it is to talk and interact with friends in a cosy, softly lit café than in the middle of a brash, noisy shopping mall. Or study in a library rather than on a rush-hour train. It's even more important for toddlers, who do not have the chance to get up and move if their surroundings are dull or stressful – they have to put up with what's on offer, often for day after day, month after month.

A toddler's environment is what gives him experience of the world. Every minute of the day, he interacts with it and learns from it. He learns that the floor is hard and shiny, but cushions are soft and nice to fall on. He learns that the windows are bright with daylight in the morning and much darker in the afternoon. He learns that the traffic noise from outside gets much louder sometimes and can even make it hard to think. He learns which noises make him jump and which make him feel calm.

Some parents turn their homes entirely over to their toddlers. That seems a little extreme to many people, but there is quite a bit you can do to adjust your home modestly to make it a rich learning environment for a toddler. Ideally, you could dedicate a room as a nursery entirely to him. But failing that, you can adapt corners of shared rooms.

Outdoor experiments

If you have an outside space that can be adapted for your toddler (or updated from being a baby garden), you might like to include:

- Areas for sitting, standing and climbing, with different levels made from logs to encourage clambering, with clean sand and sawdust underneath for safety.
- A dirt-digging spot for a toddler to dig away at the earth to hunt for creepy-crawlies and worms.
- Grassy area for rolling and water games.
- Sand box for making castles and moats.
- Sensory corner planted with a rich variety of plants a toddler can play with and sniff, such as waving grass and soft herbs.
- Trees for shade.
- Flowers and non-toxic berry plants to attract butterflies and birds.
- Child-safe water feature and wind chimes.

Toddler space

A good toddler space provides a mix of interesting objects, textures and physical challenges, but doesn't overwhelm him with choice or pose risks to his safety. It has to be a comfortable space for you, too, since your presence is crucial. The very first priority is to get rid of clutter. If the space is filled with tables and chairs and other things, a toddler will find it hard to move around and explore. It's not always easy to interact with him quickly, either, in a furniture jungle. Keep it simple so that you can easily introduce new, surprise elements and keep it safe. Toddlers are forever sticking their fingers in here, tugging at that, climbing up, and pulling things down. Make the space as risk-free as possible, so you are happy to let him explore in his own way, without strings of warnings and 'Don't...!'. Ideally, the space should work very much from a toddler's point of view, so get down on the floor and look at things from his perspective. Chairs and tables should be toddler-sized, so he can safely use them by himself. Everything you don't want him to touch must be completely out of reach.

The space needs to be well-lit, well-ventilated, clean and warm. Encourage him into good habits by making clearing up and tidying away part of every play session. Help him to understand that this is his space and it's up to him to look after it. Use interesting containers such as woven baskets with lids, stacking boxes, clear boxes, shoeboxes, wooden trays and things that he will enjoy pulling out and putting away. Organize

> Have bought Sophie her own pile of cushions from the charity shop, so she can climb or paint on them to her heart's content. #gowiththeflow

the space according to different things your toddler might do. You could cut peek-a-boo dividers in the shelf supports, or attach a mirror just out of sight behind the containers, so he catches a surprise glimpse of himself every now and then. Remember to include places where he can safely be boisterous, throwing things or jumping and banging.

Special areas

You can dedicate particular parts of the space to different kinds of play and reflection. Toddlers love having access to some sort of 'gym', which might simply mean hanging materials for grasping, pulling and kicking. Give him things to make 'mountains' from too, such as mattresses, platforms, blocks, steps and boxes for climbing on. Encourage him to play peek-a-boo and hide-and-seek by introducing boxes and dividers with holes. Make a music area by providing anything that makes a noise, from drums and chimes to whistles, shakers and old musical instruments.

Make some space for your toddler to mess around with objects of different textures – hard, smooth, corrugated, scratchy and so on. Piles of soft toys – especially animals – can be used for all sorts of games, from make-believe tea parties to adventures with animal friends. Put some other items for pretend play nearby, such as old clothes and hats, fabrics, props and items that can be transformed by the imagination.

Even if you wanted to, you probably couldn't stop your toddler scribbling on the wall. So why not make a big space that seems to invite him to scribble, with a wipe-down surface and crayons or markers to hand? Encourage him to photograph each piece, so that when you wipe them off it doesn't seem you don't value them. Write a few simple words beside each picture that may make sense to him. Make new additions to the pictures and writing every now and then and encourage him to ask for new pictures for his wall. Lastly, don't forget to give him a whole heap of books to look at on his own and with you for inspiration.

Condensed idea
A safe and stimulating environment in part of your home will function brilliantly as a dedicated learning space

(35) Being curious

As babies find their feet and become mobile, they are naturally curious and want to get into just about everything. This sometimes causes parents concern, but a baby's curiosity is what drives him to explore the world and engage confidently with it.

Seekers

Curiosity is what drives all animals to learn about the world, not just human babies. Some curiosity, known by behavioural psychologists as 'extrinsic explorative behaviour', is driven by seeking a reward. But the curiosity of babies is mostly 'intrinsic' – they explore for the sheer joy of getting to know about the world. You only have to look at the delighted concentration of a toddler grappling with a new toy, or crawling into unexpected spaces, to see how true this is.

Some psychologists suggest that there are three steps involved in a toddler's curiosity. First is 'uncertainty reduction'. This about getting to know more about unfamiliar things – how they feel, what shape they are, how heavy they are. You'll see this happening when your baby picks up an unfamiliar object, such as a squeezy bottle, and examines it. Second comes 'incorporation', where he works out how to incorporate the object into his world – he'll discover uses for it, such as squirting water, or banging it to make a noise. Third comes play, which is the creative use of the object; your baby might begin to create new realities for the squeezy bottle, such as pretending it's a spaceship. This third stage can get lost when parents are over-anxious or toddlers feel insecure. As John Bowlby showed with attachment theory (see pages 24–27), secure toddlers, who feel confident about the support and proximity of their mum or

other caregiver, follow their curiosity to explore their world boldly and thoroughly. Insecure toddlers, however, often have trouble exploring because they have not developed a feeling of security from the 'safe base' that is a reliable, predictable mum or dad.

Don't be a barrier

Curiosity has been shown to be important in everything from motivating people to develop high-achieving careers to attracting a spouse. Some studies have shown that children who were very responsive to new stimuli as infants scored higher on creativity tests aged nine than average children. Another showed that curiosity and conscientiousness are as important as intelligence in achieving high grades. So the benefits of stimulating curiosity are plain. Yet it is surprising how many of even the best-intentioned parents unwittingly stifle curiosity. Fear is one barrier to being curious about the world, and a parent who unconsciously presents the world as a dangerous place may induce a sense of fear in her toddler that will deter him from exploring. Disapproval is another barrier: a toddler who is continually told 'Don't do that!' will quickly lose curiosity and may even become anxious. Absence is a third barrier: toddlers need the reassuring presence of an adult to set out on explorations and share their discoveries.

Be curious together

Children, like adults, need to share their discoveries, so make exploration a shared activity and enjoy everything that your child finds out. Show him how fascinating the world really is by your own curiosity in the

Ways to encourage curiosity

The most important thing is to be there for your child, to give him the secure attachment he needs from day one – so that when he starts crawling and walking, he'll be curious to explore. Reassure him as he does so, while making sure he's always safe (such as by attaching gates to stairs and plastic guards to table corners and other sharp edges). If your little one is nervous about exploring, don't pressure him or the situation will worsen; concentrate on supporting him and showing that the world is a safe place, and in time his curiosity will kick in. Toddlers' curiosity can get them into all kinds of trouble and create all kinds of mess, and it's easy to dampen their enthusiasm as you worry about what they might get their hands into or put in their mouths or pull down on top of them. Resist the temptation to leap in or disapprove. Redirect, rather than discourage. Let him be in control and discover things for himself whenever it's safe to do so.

things around you. Turn everyday events into gentle adventures. When you're going shopping, for instance, take the time to look at people and things, and enjoy the splashy noise

> I've discovered Jack has a strange passion for stars. So we went to the planetarium and both loved it! #stargazer

of puddles. But don't force your own interests on him. When you go to the zoo, he might be more interested in the ants on the ground than the camels and the lions. And why not? They are interesting!

Every toddler has his own particular interests and way of exploring. Try to identify these and encourage them. He may not like messy nature or outdoor physical exploration. If so, try to discover what he does like, and find ways of helping him with that. Maybe it's music and sounds. Maybe it's the messy properties of food. Remember, too, that things change.

Once a toddler starts exploring, it's not long before he starts asking questions – probably thousands of them. Sometimes they'll be asked when you're trying to get ready for an outing or busy with a deadline, but try to be patient and answer as encouragingly as you can, so he continues to be curious and ask on other occasions. However, don't always give your answer straightaway; try to find out what he thinks first. It encourages your child to wonder if he has the answer and what it might be, while knowing that you're there as back-up. Encourage him to think and help him if he needs pointers. And if you don't know the answer, say so and let him join in the fun of finding out what it could be.

Condensed idea
Encouraging curiosity will help your toddler engage confidently with the world around him

36 Independently minded

Knowing when to hold back and let your little toddler make her own mistakes can be difficult for parents. But just as you instinctively let her stumble occasionally when she's learning to walk, so it is with many things as she gradually finds her own way of being and doing.

'Me do it!'

Babies go through three stages of dependence as they grow. In the first year a baby is totally dependent on her parents to do almost everything for her. In the second year, as a toddler, she will begin to do many things by herself, especially if she receives the right kind of encouragement. Finally, she learns to be rationally interdependent – maintaining independence when appropriate, but also appreciating that some things are better done with your help.

The stage of growing independence that typically begins in the second year is a difficult time for both parents and toddler. It's so tempting to intervene when she does make a mistake, or help her when she can't get things at first. It's natural to want to look after her. And from her point of view she wants to be independent and do things for herself, but she has no idea what's appropriate and what's not, and so all too often toddlers get into those bouts of awkwardness and even tantrums that characterize the 'terrible twos'. It can be disconcerting and even upsetting when your little angel suddenly turns into a little terror who looks at you defiantly and slams the door when you ask her to leave it open. But it is worth remembering that it is a natural part of her necessary search for independence, and in time most toddlers will move on to the stage of mature interdependence and become your sweetie again.

Finding her own way

All babies respond in different ways to the dilemma of wanting mum while also wanting to do everything for themselves. To worried onlookers, some seem desperately 'clingy', hanging on to mum's legs or running to her at every chance. Others venture boldly into the world with a recklessness that seems almost as worrying. There is no one right prescription for fostering independence, but the golden rule is to let her do it in her own sweet time. Trying to get a clingy toddler, for instance, into fending for herself before she's ready is likely to increase her sense that the world is a fearful place where she might even lose your protection. In this case, remain sensitive to her needs and gradually encourage her to do things for herself. If she encounters a problem while playing, for instance, she may cry out for help. Hesitate before rushing in; acknowledge her reassuringly and ask, 'Can you do it, honey?' That may be all she needs to solve the problem herself. If she starts to fuss from across the other side of the room, you might just let her know soothingly that she's heard, rather than sweeping her up straight away. In time, you can just be the place she comes to recharge her emotional energy – and when she does need 'you' time, give it to her clearly and fully, so she knows it's there if ever she wants it.

Be wary of saying 'No' too often (because this discourages independence) or giving your toddler no alternatives (which may be met with stubborn resistance). Give her two or more choices,

How to handle resistance

As toddlers become independent, they can become very resistant, too. They may refuse requests and deliberately do what they have been asked not to do. They may sulk, shout, and even throw things or hit and bite people. You can't stop this; it's part of growing up for many children. But you can help your toddler through this tricky patch:

- Keep calm and don't let any behaviour upset you.
- Let your toddler see that you are not fazed by her resistance, but respond clearly when she yields.
- Try to find out what the problem is: ask her, and show her you understand, if you do.
- Avoid introducing new routines and ideas at difficult times.
- Don't force strangers and strange situations on her.
- When she gets stroppy, see if you can divert her attention.
- She may be especially tricky when she's ill, so make things as easy for her as you can.
- Give her choices rather than things she can say 'no' to.

any of which is acceptable to you, and then let her choose. For example, show her a banana, apple and some other fruits and let her choose which one she'd like to eat by pointing to it. That way she can practise and grow confident at making her own decisions. Giving her choices is a great way to offer diversions rather than resorting to ultimatums when you're faced with tricky situations. For instance, if your toddler is getting cross because another child is on the swing at the park, suggest that she could go on the slide or roundabout and ask, which would she prefer? This encourages good decision making while preventing an argument.

Self-help

There are many ways you can encourage a toddler to do things for herself. The trick is to step back, even when you're sure you could do them faster and with less mess; be patient and let her do them. She will often get them wrong, but she'll also gradually learn to get them right. At mealtimes, encourage your child to start feeding herself as soon as it feels right. Give her finger foods along with cups, bowls and utensils that are easy for her to use, and allow her to make a mess before you step in with wipes or spoonfeed her yourself. In the morning see how much she can do to dress

> I've found the only way to beat the spoon-banging headache is to join in! #beatitbaby

and undress herself. Try small tasks initially: ask her to pull up her pants after you change her, or to pull her socks off when she goes to bed, for instance. She may have trouble with zips and buttons at first, so look for clothes that are elasticated or just pull-on, so she can experiment herself.

As soon as your toddler is ready, help her to tend to her own hygiene and toileting. Show her how to wash her own hands. When she's about 18 months or so, she'll be ready for potty training. Leave the potty somewhere she can see it and explore for herself. Show her what it's for, and make it easier for her to realize when she needs it by leaving off her nappy at times she's likely to need a wee. If she messes up, just clear it up and encourage her to try again next time. When she finally gets it right, acknowledge it with a little gentle praise.

Condensed idea
In the second year, a toddler needs to develop her independence by trial and (lots of) error

(37) An organized mind

You may want to scream when your toddler keeps on dropping things or rolling a car to and fro, to and fro along the same bit of floor. But this toddler 'on repeat' may actually be following a schema – a pattern of behaviour that teaches him a lot about the world.

Putting the world in order

The idea of schemas originated with Jean Piaget in the 1920s and was later developed in nursery practice by British child-development expert Chris Athey. Piaget regarded schemas as the building blocks of intelligent behaviour and a way for the brain to organize its knowledge of the world. He argued that children come to understand the world around them by finding patterns (schemas) in it, which they realize by seeing certain things repeated over and over again. This allows the patterns to be categorized, classified and better understood – then applied to everyday situations. A child might begin to see, for instance, that some things move to and fro, while others go inside things.

> Tom keeps putting a cloth over his face to make himself invisible. Must not laugh. #scientistmum

A schema, then, is a pattern of thought or behaviour that allows children to make sense of the world. It's likely that the very same repeated patterns of behaviour that prove so annoying to parents are actually attempts by a baby or toddler to master a particular kind of movement or symbolic concept. Adults use schemas too; we follow set routines for particular situations, such as ordering a meal in a restaurant. We don't wonder each time how to move through the various stages involved – we have already learned them and hold them as a workable concept in our brains. But for toddlers, Piaget argued, schemas are their principal way of learning about the world. It's why, for instance, an older baby, having grasped that four-legged animals are cats, might go to the zoo and point to an elephant and say 'cat!' with the pleasure of recognition.

Piaget identified definite stages in a child's development, and so particular schemas have become identified with particular stages in a child's life. Many nursery guides on schemas stress this developmental

Developmental stages

Jean Piaget's insight was to realize that children cannot perform certain tasks until they are psychologically ready to. He suggested there are particular psychological milestones:

- **Sensorimotor stage (birth–2 years)**: differentiates self from objects; recognizes self as agent of action and begins to act intentionally.
- **Pre-operational stage (2–7 years)**: learns language and to represent objects by images and words; finds it hard to see the viewpoint of others; classifies objects by a single feature.
- **Concrete operational stage (7–11 years)**: thinks logically about objects and events; understands how number, mass and weight operate; classifies things using several features.
- **Formal operational stage (11 years and up)**: can think logically about abstract ideas and test theories systematically; becomes interested in the future and ideals.

linkage. Early schemas are based on essentially simple movement and sense based notions, while later toddler versions include more advanced ideas such as pretend play and understanding cause and effect. Since Piaget's time, the details of his developmental stages have been called into question by later psychologists, but the idea of schemas has grown and developed. In practical terms, they represent a very useful way of working with your toddler rather than against him.

Looking for schemas

If you understand that your toddler is not simply being annoying but repeating experiments and trying different variations on a theme until he is sure of the result, you can see him as a truly diligent scientist – and you can assist him in his work rather than try to divert him to something else (which might cause both you and him frustration). Watch him carefully and try to identify any schema he is following through the patterns of behaviour he is repeating. If his interest is in carrying things, don't give him a spade and encourage him to dig when he's in the sandpit – give him a bucket to carry the sand. That way he's much more likely to respond and to learn something.

Common schemas

One of the earliest schemas is called 'trajectory'; it seems to develop from a toddler's pleasure in being rocked to and fro. When testing this, a toddler might like running toy cars back and forth, or lining things up. Or he might run to and fro repeatedly or jump up and down. Or he might throw things – or, more annoyingly, drop things! When he's mastered this one, he might move on to one of the most common schemas, known as 'enveloping'. While building this schema, a toddler might wrap teddy in a blanket, cover his face with a towel, enjoy wrapping presents, become especially interested in tunnels and dens or even, surprisingly, paint all over a picture he's just done with one colour.

There are many types of schema. If your child becomes fascinated by how things go inside each other, he's working on 'containing'. He'll keep on moving things in and out of boxes, trolleys, bags and so on, to see them appear and disappear. He may even want to try containing himself, climbing into boxes and cupboards. Or he may seem to become fixated with the idea of how things are moved from one place to another, when coming to grips with 'transporting'. He might put things in bags and carry them to and fro, or take charge of the pushchair and use it to transport things. Some toddlers like nothing better than crashing cars through a wall they've built, or bursting through a pile of cushions. These children are testing 'boundary breaking'. Others may exhibit the endless capacity to study 'rotating' and will love watching washing machines, playing with toys with wheels, rolling down hills, and being spun round. So if you find yourself scratching your head in bemusement at some strangely repetitive behaviour, rest assured that it's actually great learning.

Condensed idea
Repeated patterns of behaviour can show you what schema your child scientist is working on right now

38 Arty party

Creativity is one of the most valuable skills a child can learn. Not every child will grow up to be an artistic genius, but creativity is about the ability to think about new ideas and that's something that every child can benefit from. However, it's a skill that needs nurturing.

What is creativity?

Experts disagree about just what creativity is. It's not quite the same as intelligence or talent. Indeed, children who score highly in intelligence tests are not necessarily creative and vice versa. Most child development experts agree, though, that while it's hard to pin down exactly what creativity is, with children in particular it's about far more than the arts and music. It's about imagination, originality (the ability to come up with new ideas), productivity (the ability to work through ideas), problem solving, and the ability to create something of value.

The 'Reggio Emilia approach', which originated in the villages around the Italian town of Reggio Emilia after World War 2, emphasizes that with young children, creativity is all about 'process'. We should not see a child's creativity in what she produces, but in how she goes about it. At certain life stages, a child will not have the necessary skills to create something special, but that doesn't mean that her approach is not highly creative. As Loris Malaguzzi, the creator of the Reggio Emilia movement,

> Doing arty stuff with Ethan is making me come up with better solutions at work! #creativitycog

said: 'Creativity becomes more visible when adults try to be more attentive to the cognitive processes of children than to the results they achieve in various fields of doing and understanding.'

Nurturing the artist

Creativity seems to need nurturing. A toddler will need some gentle encouragement to think creatively. She needs help to realize that open-ended questions like 'What's teddy going to do tomorrow?' are exciting openings for the imagination. She needs guidance to see that there is not just one way of putting on your clothes – there can be many, each equally valid. She needs encouragement to try things out, and praise when she comes up with a surprising answer or result of her own. She needs positive feedback on the way she is going about things. And above all, she needs to know her efforts (not just results) are valued.

It is very easy to stifle creativity. A child may learn to avoid creative thinking, for instance, because she starts to believe she hasn't anything worth offering. She may feel exposed when confronted with a situation

in which there is no neat solution. Or she may feel that her chosen way of self-expression is somehow bad – if she is told, for instance, that getting things covered in paint is dirty, or singing is much too noisy. It's so easy to give out these negative messages unwittingly as you wipe up quickly after her mess, or continually say 'Ssh!' when she starts banging loudly on a drum. Some limits do need to be placed on unbridled self-expression, but it's important for a toddler to learn these in a positive way, through choice rather than fear of getting things wrong. Check from time to time that you're not giving out these negative messages.

Boosting creativity

Besides encouraging your toddler to think for herself, there are all kinds of things you can do to encourage her creativity. Many of us think of art-based activities first, but remember that budding scientists need imagination and innovative skills too, and all forms of creativity count.

One way of encouraging creativity is to help your child make her own toys. You could make a ship from an old plastic box and get her to paint on the portholes, or a doll's house from a shoebox, or binoculars from two toilet rolls, and so on. While cooking, let her help you in the kitchen as much as you can. Give her the chance to mix ingredients and see them change. Get a simple infant's recipe book and give her some starter ideas for her own recipes – but don't insist she follows what it says in the book. If it's a disaster, that's all part of the process.

Children love make-believe, so fertilize your toddler's imagination by filling a 'busy box' with all kinds of things that don't have an obvious purpose but can be used imaginatively, such as blocks, paper plates, old cups, plastic bottles, pieces of cloth, old hats and much more. Show her how a paper plate could be a steering wheel and make up a story about it. Let her try things out for herself. Encourage her to make up stories, by using, say, a block of wood as a sailing boat. Ask questions, such as 'What's that you've got? Is it a boat?' and 'Where's it sailing to?'. Don't be tempted to make up the stories yourself!

Ideas for hours of fun and learning

Toddlers love arty play, and the ones given below will maximize the creative learning for your child:

- **Sponge painting:** cut kitchen sponges into different shapes and let your toddler dip them into tempera paint and dab them on all kinds of surfaces – boxes, bags, paper or anything else you're happy for her to paint.
- **String painting:** collect some short bits of string and old shoelaces and dip them in paint for her to make patterns with – keep her under a watchful eye, though.
- **Crayons and paper:** find some chunky, easy-to-grip crayons, then tear up some old paper bags or bits of paper for her to scrawl on. Tape the paper to the table to make it easier.
- **Collages:** you can stick just about anything on paper to build up a picture: snippings of fabric and wool, torn-up paper, bits of magazines, food wrappers – or, take inspiration from nature, and give her sand, acorns, seeds, twigs, leaves and more.
- **Colouring books:** there's a huge range of these books for infants, from magic painting books in which colours appear as you wet the paper to activity books with join-the-dots and colouring-in puzzles.

Condensed idea
Creativity is vital to innovation, problem solving and brilliant thinking

Music is one of the most wonderful things you can give to a toddler. It's a source of comfort, joy and excitement. It also helps stimulate the development of brain connections in a wide variety of ways. Children who gain an early love of music tend to keep it forever.

In tune with ourselves and others

Music is now an unavoidable part of our lives, and most people agree that there is magic in it. In his *Music Talks with Children*, the 19th-century German poet Berthold Auerbachin said that 'Music washes away from the soul the dust of everyday life', while German philosopher and composer Friedrich Nietzsche insisted, 'Without music, life would be a mistake'. For little children, music seems to have very special powers.

Even young toddlers love songs that include counting up or down, or making hand gestures

A few years ago it was suggested that playing Mozart to unborn babies turned them into intellectual powerhouses (see page 19). While this is now considered unlikely, the benefits of music are plain. Emotional regulation (learning how to prevent one's emotions becoming overwhelming) is an essential skill, and even a newborn will be soothed by lullabies. These help a baby to calm down, and as they do so on repeated occasions, he begins to learn to calm himself. Music also helps children identify and control emotions – babies as young as five months respond differently to happy and sad music. This is especially important for toddlers, who are only just beginning to learn what emotions are.

Music helps build bonds, too. As a shared activity, it builds connections in a way that few other activities do. If a toddler is singing or making music with you or in a group, he will try to find the same melody and the same rhythm. He's making an effort to be in tune with you or his peers. Toddlers tend to play by themselves when they first go to nursery groups, and singing together may be the first time that they experience 'peer play' – doing something together with others of their own age. There are few things more delightful than seeing a group of toddlers in a nursery banging drums, clapping their hands and trying to sing along together.

Learning sequences

There are cognitive benefits in music, too, as it introduces patterns and sequences, counting and symbolic ideas. Repetitive songs such as 'Old MacDonald Had a Farm' are wonderful at reinforcing patterns and sequences. So too are call-and-response songs like 'A Farmer Did a-Hunting Go'. Getting the beat by clapping, tapping and patting seems to help give toddlers a sense of control that can have psychological benefits. In addition, the language benefits come through repeating words, picking out rhymes and phonemes (word sounds), practising emphases and learning about turn-taking. There are also marked physical benefits to music-making: toddlers will develop their gross motor skills as they sway and stamp to the music and perhaps even dance, as well as their fine motor skills as they play with toy drumsticks and musical instruments.

Toddler orchestra

There's now a huge range of instruments available for toddlers, but you don't need anything very elaborate to start making music. Toddlers are really only capable of banging and shaking, so there are lots of instruments you can make yourself. These are the basic essentials of a toddlers' orchestra:

- Maracas and shakers are great for the youngest toddlers, as they make a noise however they are moved. Make them from plastic bottles filled with dried rice or peas.
- Rhythm sticks (simply sticks!) can be banged together for a pleasing clunky sound.
- Toddlers love banging things and there are lots of toddlers' drums available, from kettle drums to bongos, but an upturned pot and a wooden spoon can be just as good.
- Jingle bells are great for younger toddlers. They can be sewn onto Velcro® strips that can be attached to his wrist or ankle.
- Tambourines take a little skill to use, but older toddlers can have hours of fun with these.

What kind of song?

Toddlers like short songs or songs with short verses. Their memories are not fully developed, and a short song delivers quickly. Most toddlers love songs with actions, and these are especially good for them, because the actions help them remember the words as well as giving them practice with motor skills. Make the most of songs you hear on the radio or just make up yourself by accompanying them with movements such as jumping, swinging, twisting or shaking an arm, leg or your head. Some toddlers will need plenty of time and gentle encouragement before they understand what to do, so be patient. Gently try singing and dancing with your toddler from time to time, and be ready to help him join in when he shows signs of wanting to do so.

Look for songs that help develop particular skills in turn. For instance, songs that encourage physical skills, such as 'Heads, Shoulders, Knees and Toes', or thinking songs like 'One Two, Buckle my Shoe'. Or songs that stretch language by getting toddlers to fill in the blanks, such as 'Old MacDonald', or encourage imaginative play, like 'Baa Baa Black Sheep'. Ask your toddler to act out the

> Just spent an hour singing 'Old MacDonald' with Noah and his wooden farm animals. Never laughed so much. #lovetosing

song and dance with toys. Search out songs and music for singing and playing together (with parents, family or friends) to build up social and emotional skills. Musical statues, in which you stop the music and get your toddler to stand still until the music starts again, are fun and good for practising self-control.

Toddlers love it when you sing with them, but it's also useful to have child-friendly recordings to play from time to time when you run out of inspiration. This can still be a shared activity. In fact, music can be incorporated into lots of areas of your child's life, not just specific music times. You can even make up little songs to help him remember routines, like washing or dressing – the sequencing of the music will help him remember the sequence involved in the task at hand.

Condensed idea
Music has social, emotional, cognitive, physical and language benefits

40 Hold that thought

One of the best ways of developing your toddler's thinking skills is through a shared process of enquiry known as 'sustained shared thinking'. This involves being aware of a toddler's interests and working together with her to develop an idea or skill.

The brain nursery

The idea that adult-child interactions are important in developing thinking skills is not new. It's at the centre of the Russian psychologist Lev Vygotsky's ideas from the 1920s, but it gained a great boost a decade or so ago when Iram Siraj-Blatchford, a British professor of childhood education, drew attention to the value of 'sustained shared thinking' in UK nurseries. The studies in which Siraj-Blatchford was involved showed that the nurseries getting the best results (producing the most cognitively developed, happiest children) were those in which the infants and staff worked together to solve problems and answer questions. Interestingly, the studies showed that highly qualified staff were the most effective at developing this interactive approach with their little charges.

'Our investigations of adult-child interaction', wrote Siraj-Blatchford, 'have led us to the view that periods of 'sustained shared thinking' are a necessary prerequisite for the most effective early years practice, especially where this is also encouraged in the home through parents' support.' This means that if your toddler is at a nursery that follows the practice of sustained shared thinking, you can support their work at home by adopting a similar approach. However, it is also a really valuable approach for you to take independently at home, whether your child attends nursery or not.

The basic idea is for carer and child to work together to stretch and develop the child's thinking, especially on a one-to-one basis. Siraj-Blatchford defined sustained shared thinking as an episode in which two or more individuals 'work together' in an intellectual way to solve a problem, clarify a concept, evaluate activities or extend a narrative, for example. The key thing is that both people must contribute to the thinking and it must develop and extend. So making up a story together or working out the best thing to use as a door-stop (and why) are equally great ways of practising sustained shared thinking.

How does it work?

The power of sustained shared thinking is based on the fact that little children get very excited by learning and discovery. They are genuinely motivated when they feel they are learning something for themselves, because they feel like adventurous explorers in the world of ideas and knowledge. What kills their excitement is being 'taught' things.

Open questions

Sustained shared thinking works best with open questions. There are a few that seem to work well in most situations and these may be worth remembering:

- I wonder what would happen if we...?
- How did you...?
- Why does this...?
- Do you think you could...?
- Could you find a way to...?
- What happens next?
- How could we find out if...?
- What do you think is going on here?
- I don't know, what do you think?

One way this works is through using open questions. A closed question is one with a right or wrong answer. For instance, 'Is this animal a lion?' is a closed question. The toddler can only answer 'yes' or 'no' and his interest soon wanes. An open question might be 'What kind of animal do you think this is?'. The child's answer might prompt the adult to then ask, 'Why do you think so?', continuing the line of thought. This allows the toddler space to expand on what she thinks might make a lion or a tiger, and much more. It expands what the two people are thinking about and the possibilities and ideas attached to all sorts of concepts.

Rising to the challenge

Asking questions that your toddler will respond to in a way that promotes her intellectual adventure is far from easy. It's tempting and easy to offer her an answer or 'lead' her answers without realizing it.

So sustained shared thinking requires a little practice. The thing to remember is that this is not a journey your toddler can go on by herself. While it centres on her getting the excitement and mental stimulation of pursuing her own answers, it's a mutual journey and she needs you to keep opening the way for her. In this way it's a challenge for you, too, and a highly

> We've just worked out five reasons why bees might make honey. All good! #teamplayer

rewarding one – in which both you and your toddler can get such a buzz that you just have to tell people what you worked out today! To really make it work, you have to tune in to your toddler's responses, watch her body language and try to see what she might be thinking about. You have to sustain a real interest in her answers and respect the choices she makes, even if you think she might be way off beam. You need to share your own ideas respectfully, recapping and clarifying to show you've understood what she's been saying and how she's sparked your thinking. Every now and then, you might want to remind her of something she's said earlier, such as 'You said my feet would get wet if I stepped in that puddle – and look at my boots now!'.

The idea is to help your toddler plan and speculate: to solve problems and work things out, to reason and use logic to understand and find answers, to explore creatively using imagination, and to reflect on and resolve conflicting feelings as they arise. Help her keep up the momentum and feel that your joint line of inquiry is really going somewhere. Get excited about what the two of you are doing – there's no limit to the learning.

Condensed idea
Take every opportunity to do some shared thinking with your child, wondering about how things are and might become

(41) Vocabulary explosion

After struggling to manage just a word or two, at about 18 months many toddlers suddenly learn scores of new words and even phrases. You can make the most of this sudden fountain of words in several ways, and really help your toddler develop her language skills.

Word burst

There's no doubt that toddlers understand words long before they can say them, which is why they take so readily to baby signing (see pages 100–103). Even at nine months, a baby might respond with understanding when you make an animal noise, or try to make the noise themselves. At around one year old, a typical toddler understands about 50 words, and goes on to learn a new word or so every day for the next three months. By 15 months, most toddlers have learned the significance of pointing to an object (they realize that it indicates an instruction to look from an outstretched arm in a continuing direction), and at this point they begin to point at objects for adults to name. This speeds up the vocabulary process, and they start to learn around two new words a day, so by 18 months of age they can understand perhaps 180 words. These are likely to include nouns (such as 'dog'); verbs (such as 'sleep' and 'go'); location words (such as 'down' and 'in'); and greetings (such as 'hello' and 'bye-bye'). Many toddlers even understand phrases such as 'Do you want more?' and 'Don't do that!'.

Yet however much they understand, young toddlers can say little because they haven't yet developed the right vocal muscle control to mimic the words they hear – this is the big change that happens at what experts call the 'vocabulary explosion'. It's not that a toddler has just learned all the words that suddenly start pouring from her mouth – it's that she's just worked out how to say them. Typically, this happens at about 18 months, but every child is different, and it may occur at any age from 15 months to three years, or even later. Girls are, on average, slightly earlier than boys, but the difference between individuals is much greater. First-borns are also slightly earlier, too. The implication is obvious – babies learn earlier when their parents talk more to them (and have time to talk to them), especially in an encouraging way.

Be a translator

You'll notice the explosion begin when your toddler starts to learn a few dozen words and use them in the right situation. Then suddenly, she'll start to say hundreds of words and perhaps even string together phrases. It's at this point that you can really help (or hinder) your toddler's progress. She may make mistakes. She may call the neighbours' cat 'doggy' while she works out the exact concept attached to the word. Does 'doggy' refers to all shaggy moving animals? Or four-legged pets? When

Word outings

If your baby sees the same things around the home and does not go out very much, her vocabulary will stall – so take her out as often as you can on little trips to show her new experiences and objects to be named. Take her to the park, for instance, and ask her to pick up flowers, pebbles and twigs. Name them for her, there and then. Ask her which ones she likes best and why, then suggest that she chooses a few things to take home with her (with a little steering towards smaller objects!). Then she can practise saying the words again at home.

you're correcting her, be positive – a negative correction will rob her of confidence. Encourage her efforts and try to work out the analogy she's seen; say something like 'Yes, yes! It is a man like dada! This man is the postman, the post – man. He brings us the post'.

Sometimes, the sound your toddler comes out with may not be a recognizable word. She may say 'bobob' when she wants some juice, for instance. You might later guess that she's trying to say 'bottle'. It doesn't matter that it's not right, as long as you show her that her efforts are appreciated and (usually!) understood. Very soon, your toddler will begin to put words together in her own combinations and attempt to master grammar. This is an astonishing achievement, because it means far more than mimicking – it's creating entirely new combinations to convey a message of her own. If Sasha says 'Sasawawa' ('Sasha water') when she wants to paddle, it is a much bigger achievement than saying 'Sleepy time' perfectly – because she has created speech to convey her intention; it is not just something that she has heard you say. She's combining things from memory and imagination.

Talk the talk

Babies who are talked to a lot develop language skills faster than others, so the most important thing you can do to help your baby or toddler is to talk to her. You don't need to chatter all the time, but engage her in conversation whenever you can. Tell her what you're doing. Point things out. Sing songs and recite nursery rhymes. Listen to her efforts to talk too, and give her the reward of showing you understand whenever you do – even if you don't quite! Eye contact maintains engagement, and so is extremely valuable when talking to your baby or toddler. It lets her know that she's involved.

> Just been told at length by toddler what her teddy wants for lunch. Can't help thinking maybe toddler does too. #chatterbox

When it comes to conversations, let your toddler lead the way. Allow her to choose the topics to talk about, because that way she'll be interested and want to drive the talk forward. Give her some new words about that topic because her interest will increase her desire to learn. If she loves cats, show and name a cat's whiskers, paws, fur and tail, for instance.

Children who are asked a lot of questions start to ask a lot of questions, enabling them to progress cognitively and linguistically. So ask questions that require her to think, but are not so vague that she doesn't know where to start. Ask, for instance, 'What was the story daddy told you today?' rather than, 'What did you do today?'. Always try to understand rather than correct her if she gets it wrong. She'll soon begin to correct her own mistakes and confidence is everything when it comes to talking.

Condensed idea
If you listen carefully to your toddler and make a real effort to understand, she'll quickly become a brilliant speaker

(42) Screened out

We live in a media-dominated world and it's hard to keep a toddler away from TV, smartphone and computer technology even if you want to. This chapter looks at how you can use technology in valuable ways, making the most of its educational benefits.

Media world

Babies arrive in a media-frantic world. In 2009, a survey showed that 99 per cent of homes in the USA had TVs, 73 per cent had computers and 63 per cent had internet access. Given the prevalence of smart phones and tablets, that proportion is probably even higher today. What's more, two-thirds of US households have TV on half the time and one in three have it on all the time. So even if babies aren't watching TV, they have it as a constant background, drawing their attention or that of the adults in the house. This runs against the advice of the American Academy of Pediatrics, which recommends that children under two should watch no TV at all. They cite research which suggests that children under two are not able to understand the content at that age, so educational claims for programmes for this age are false.

What's wrong with TV?

Other scientists take a more moderate line. Nonetheless, there is general consensus that for the under-twos, too much TV is a bad thing. First, it deprives babies and toddlers of the interaction with adults that is so vital at this age for healthy brain development. Second, it causes confusion through a primitive reflex called the 'orienting response'. When a toddler seems glued to the screen, it is less likely to be genuine fascination than this ancient reflex, which makes a human focus on a sudden sight or sound in case it's a threat. Fast-edit, exciting programmes tend to stimulate this response more than others and may lead to children expecting to feel it all the time; it is thought that this may lead to attention lapses later

> Love Grandpa and Tom spending time together, but wish it wasn't on the iPad! #screeningmum

in life. A third problem is that when the TV is on in the background, its chatter makes it harder for toddlers to process other sounds around them, so may delay language learning.

It's not easy to decide when to turn the TV on and off, especially if you're a busy single parent. The most important things are to keep unsupervised watching time to a minimum and to turn off the TV when no one is watching it. Sharing a little carefully chosen, slow-paced TV with your toddler while you chat together about it can be genuinely rewarding.

Digital eyes

There are numerous digital cameras for toddlers and most are so simple to operate that your little one may well be able to work out how to use it without any help from you. The photo quality may not be very good, but that won't bother a child. It's exciting for a toddler to take pictures of the world around him, and will encourage him to learn the names and purpose of things.

Once you think your toddler is ready, help him make a photo album of his favourite things. These could include family members or friends, or things he's seen on walks or nature trips. When he's old enough, you could occasionally choose one letter of the alphabet and ask him to take pictures of things he can think of that begin with that letter. If you don't have a camera, try downloading and printing pictures of his favourite things from a computer. Encourage his creativity by suggesting he try doing collages or cut-outs.

Computers

Toddlers find technology fascinating, because it lets them do clever things. Most toddlers love pressing buttons, and you may find that your toddler is a little more adept at switching on the TV with the remote control or pushing buttons on a computer keyboard than you'd like. However, he's really showing that he wants to imitate you, so it might be worth finding him an old keyboard to bash on without fear of damage (virtual or otherwise). In the past, parents did not have to worry too much about a toddler's use of computers, because the under-twos don't have the manual skill to operate a mouse or enough knowledge to press the keyboard other than randomly. They may have become familiar with computers, talking to family members abroad on screen or looking at family photos, but this seems positive because it is interactive. Tablet computers, however, may have changed the situation radically.

Toddler tablets

Tablets are small and easy for a toddler to hold; the touch-screen and swipe systems are so easy to use that even babies under one can manage to use them. In addition to the wealth of baby-oriented apps for adult tablets, there are also tablets that are purpose-built for toddlers. These tend to feature child-friendly add-ons, such as big, soft, padded cases that protect the tablet from knocks and make it easy for a toddler to pick up.

Opponents of toddler tablets think that screen-time takes little ones away from interacting with the world, from physical development and from interaction with carers. Supporters argue that they're no different in essence from a clever interactive book – and they're great for parent and child to look at together. The great benefit must be that they can introduce toddlers to the computer technology that will be part of their lives at a very early age. They will become familiar with moving around the screen, finding things and finding answers within, and the right software may even help with language and cognitive skills. On the other hand, there is a genuine danger the tablet will become addictive, especially if used unsupervised, and drain away time from much more valuable activities. It's far too early yet for any conclusive research to have emerged, so for now, it seems wise to use them very judiciously – under your watchful eye and for limited periods only.

Condensed idea
Use technology to your toddler's advantage, rather than allowing it to halt his progress

43 Wired for learning

Some parents and carers fill a toddler's day with all kinds of planned activities to provide constant stimulation. But this actually runs counter to a toddler's natural way of learning – through exploration and self-chosen play – which helps him develop his own identity.

Natural adventurers

Toddlers don't learn in the same ways as older children. They are not like children aged over five, who benefit from having clear goals and a planned curriculum for learning. Toddlers are adventurers and explorers, driven by the desire for knowledge; they are always on the hunt for new sensations or some new snippet of information about the world. What they need from their carers is emotional security, physical care and models of behaviour that they can look to and try to mimic. What they don't need is a non-stop diet of lessons. American psychology professor Alison Gopnik points out that babies and toddlers are not trying to learn one particular skill or set of facts – they are drawn to anything new, unexpected or informative. As a result, what they need is not information, but the support, encouragement and confidence to make their own discoveries. This is one of the reasons why one-to-one attention is so important for toddlers: they need a sense of safety and a way to practise the free exchange of ideas.

The realization that toddlers are in fact their own best teachers, wired for seeking out the skills and knowledge they need, has led nurseries to alter their approach and make sure they schedule time for child-initiated activities. You can use these recent findings to help your child at home too. Essentially, it means that rather than trying to fill your toddler's day

with things to do, you need to clear him some space to come up with ideas of his own. By all means bring in new things and give him ideas, but let him set the agenda, while you simply act as a facilitator. You might take your toddler to a stream in a park, fondly imagining how he will paddle in the shallows or build little dams, but when you get there, find that all he wants to do is dig holes in the earth with a stick. Respect his choice; he might follow your ideas another time. What you can do – and, in fact, what he needs you to do – is take an interest in his choice and talk to him about it. Similarly, if your toddler is playing a make-believe game and you sense that he wants you involved, go along with the idea. If he's making a farm for his animals, for instance, join in the pretence by, say, arriving as a vet to look after one of the sick animals. However, only stay to play for as long as he wants you to be there.

Multi-tasking children

In the second year of their life, more than at any time, toddlers are working hard to develop their own sense of themselves. When your toddler turns round and says 'No!' when you ask him to stop throwing his food on the floor, he's not simply being difficult for the sake of it. He's doing it for several reasons. First, he's trying to form his own identity, to establish himself as a distinct individual. One of the ways he can do this is through trying out new behaviours. Second, he's trying things out, looking at the adults around him, monitoring how different behaviours go down with adults and peers. As a parent, your love is vital to him – his survival depends upon it – and he will be keeping a close eye on which behaviours seem to please you or make you angry. At the same time, he's very taken up with experimenting with the world, finding out how things work, and organizing his knowledge into various schemas (see pages 148–51). Your toddler is trying to work out who he is, who the people around him are (and what they want or expect from him), and how things in the world operate. No wonder toddlers need to set their own schedule!

A make-believe treasure box

One activity many toddlers choose for themselves if allowed to do so is playing make-believe. They like pretending to be things – such as a dog, a bus, a bird or a doctor. There is nowhere their fantasy can't lead them. If you have room, put together a box of materials that they can use to feed their imagination. Include:

- Pictures that might spark an idea.
- Things that make a funny noise.
- Pieces of fabric, old clothes and hats for dressing up.
- Toy animals, puppets and figurines for travelling companions.
- Objects such as rods, toilet rolls, plastic boxes and other intriguing potential props.

Learning about myself

According to US child development practitioner Dr J. Ronald Lally, toddlers are constantly on the look-out for things to help them forge their identity: what to be afraid of; how well adults react to particular behaviours; how adults respond to messages; how well adults meet their needs; how emotions go down with adults (both their own and the adults'); and how interested adults are in them. They forge their identity by building a picture of how they can fit into this world with these people, effectively asking 'Who can I be, with people like these, in a world like this?'. Carers play a hugely important part in shaping a toddler's personality – both in terms of their direct response to the toddler, and in the way they enable a toddler to play, explore and learn for themselves.

Toddlers may sometimes stubbornly resist your suggestions for things to do, deciding they want to play indoors when you point out how sunny it is outdoors or vice versa. But however much they revel in the freedom and self-motivation of the activities they have chosen for themselves, they still need constant feedback. When your toddler finds a worm under a stone, he wants

> Jack has invented a brilliant new game that involves his favourite biscuits. Genius! #soclever

you to know what he's discovered. It's not a question of praising him for his success, but taking a genuine interest and showing an understanding of what it means to him, so that he has the confidence and motivation to go further. Join in with his enthusiasm and see where it takes you both.

Condensed idea
Self-chosen activities help a toddler to develop his knowledge, confidence and identity

(44) Mood swings

As toddlers progress through their second year, they become aware of the power of emotions, but they don't have the brain development to keep them under control. This can lead to dramatic mood swings. Parents need to help children learn this emotional intelligence.

Ups and downs

One minute your 18-month-old seems sweetness and light, delightfully playing with her crayons and chuckling – then the next minute she turns into the little monster from hell, stamping her feet, flailing out with her arms, tearing at you and screaming at a volume that would put a howler monkey to shame. Such mood swings can be genuinely upsetting, even frightening, however many times you've been warned that most toddlers go through a stage of feeling and behaving like this.

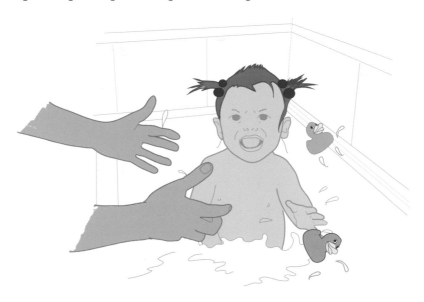

But rest assured; this is a phase that will pass. Your toddler will emerge as a calmer person in a year or so, having learned a lot about self-control. In the meantime, your task is to be your toddler's calm rock in the stormy seas that are battering her during this period of growth. One of the best ways you can help is to try to understand just why your toddler has become crotchety. This will help you to know what's really going on, acknowledge her feelings, validate them and explain to her what's happening and why. For instance, when you tell her you understand that she's upset because it's too wet to go outside, and that

> Didn't realise Aisha was scared about moving house until she started throwing screaming fits. Lots of hugs and chats are helping. #movershaker

you often feel disappointed about this too, but perhaps you could both play with her farm for a while and then see if the sun has come out, you are teaching her vital skills. This type of feedback helps her to recognize her feelings and begin to learn that they can be acknowledged and acted upon in different ways. It sows the seeds of emotional self-regulation and the recognition that other people experience mood changes too – ideas which lie at the heart of emotional intelligence.

No way!

At this age your child begins to notice emotions, but she has no idea just what it is that she's feeling. Help her build emotional intelligence by showing her what emotions are and that everyone goes through them. Read books together in which the characters go through emotions. Point out moments when the character is sad or happy, and say things like, 'Look, he's feeling sad, because…'. This means that when your toddler is sad, you can say, 'I see you're sad because…' or 'It's nice that you're happy because…' and she'll begin to understand what you mean. Go on to show how she can identify other people's emotions: 'Look, the bear's smiling because he's happy…'. Talk about your own emotions, too, and demonstrate with the appropriate face when saying things like: 'I'm so happy you put your toys away by yourself'. Many of the situations that cause the eruption of emotion involve a toddler's attempts at independence. That's why 'I can do it!' and 'No!' begin to appear so often in her repertoire. She wants to do things for herself and will fiercely resist your attempts to do them for her – but if she can't manage to do it for

Tantrums and neuroscience

The human brain takes seven years to grow in its entirety, and children under the age of five have not developed the brain structures that will allow them to self-calm in an emotional crisis. Neuroscientist Margot Sunderland claims there are two types of tantrum: the distress tantrum and the 'little Nero' tantrum.

A distress tantrum occurs when a toddler becomes overwhelmed by an emotion that she can't control. If she suddenly feels consumed by rage or fear, for instance, her body may quickly become flooded with stress hormones that will make it almost impossible for her to think or speak clearly or rationally. In this situation, the best thing to do is provide lots of reassuring hugs and comforting words.

Little Nero tantrums, on the other hand, don't normally involve tears – they spring from thwarted ambition, rather than stress. Like the emperor Nero, the toddler assumes that her wishes should be granted, and granted now! In this situation, the toddler needs to learn that she can't always have what she wants, and it's not okay to demand it from others by shouting. If your toddler becomes a little Nero, say 'No' firmly and do not reward the tantrum with attention.

herself, she will get very frustrated. She may find it really aggravating to discover she just hasn't the skill to put on her shirt by herself as she so wanted to. Tell her that you understand she wants to do things for herself and that you know how upsetting it is to find yourself thwarted. By identifying her emotion and validating it, you're teaching her a great deal; you can also help her see how to deal with a tricky emotion by showing her that she always has choices – in both what she does and how she feels. In this case, for instance, help her to find an alternative top that she can manage to put on herself, such as a slip-on T-shirt. Remember, too, that if you don't offer her a choice, often her only way to be independent is simply to say 'No'.

What's wrong?

Some of the issues are about communication. Your toddler may have a lot more words in her vocabulary now, but often she just won't have the right ones to express what she wants. The frustration at not being understood can turn her mood in seconds. So look for clues – perhaps in her gestures – to what she might mean before she gives up. Toddlers can also get fractious if there's been some kind of change (they are reassured by routines). Even coming to the end of an activity can be too abrupt for a toddler. They don't have the imagination, yet, to realize that there are other things they can enjoy after the fun thing they're doing now. Flag up in advance that you're going to stop soon, and help her prepare for it. Keep opening up her eyes to the possibilities that are inherent in or could follow the current situation. Sometimes the reason for a tantrum is less obvious – she may be reacting to feeling pressured or overstimulated. So keep your mind open to these possibilities too.

Condensed idea
Helping your toddler understand and regulate sudden emotional swings will support her emotional development

45 Cognitive development

In their first year, babies spend their time reacting almost automatically in response to sensory changes. But in the second year they start to think much more. They begin to understand things about the world and their responses become based on thought.

Little scientists

Babies are born learners and scientists, eager to learn and know about the world. As they progress into their second year, they really start to think about it. Psychologists talk about 'cognitive' (thinking) development gathering pace. Our cognitive abilities are those we use to process and store knowledge, reason, remember, solve problems, and use symbolic language (including linguistics and mathematics).

One of the big discoveries of recent years has been that we should not underestimate just how clever toddlers are. They might look clumsy as they stumble about on their short legs and they might sound barely brighter than a teddy bear as they produce their few weirdly pronounced words, but they are actually thinkers of profound insight and quickness. American psychology professor Alison Gopnik describes adults as the marketing and sales department of the human race, but babies as the R & D (Research and Development) division. Babies and toddlers are such radical thinkers

> I used to worry about Alice's imaginary friend, but have realized it's a clever way she's found for feeling safe when exploring. #letgo

that some computer scientists are beginning to study the way they think and solve problems as a way of developing new models for superfast computers. It's all about perception and connection: toddlers are very aware of what's going on around them (their minds are focused on the present, not past or future) and they are much more open to making imaginative connections than adults. When your toddler gets distracted by the colour of the wall, or sits toying with his shoelaces while you're

Changes between one and two

Every toddler develops at a different rate, but here are some random differences you may see between your child's first and second years.

A one-year-old:
- points to things he wants.
- imitates animal sounds.
- can name familiar people and things but cannot combine words.
- begins to learn the name of body parts.
- begins to use objects for their purpose.
- plays in parallel with other babies rather than together with them.
- is not sure what is pretend and what is real.
- solves problems entirely by trial and error.

A two-year-old:
- is able to follow simple instructions.
- uses objects to represent other objects.
- can combine two or more words in a sentence.
- can memorize simple rhymes and songs.
- talks about his feelings and wishes.
- begins to think about doing something before doing it.
- begins to solve problems by analysis and planning.
- wants choices but can't always make a decision.

trying to get his coat on to go out, he's not being slow, he's being a scientist and creator, wondering about that colour or those shoelaces and what they are and can do. Why are they precisely like that and not otherwise? Why does that bit of wall (in shade) look darker? As adults, we learn to shut things out and focus on goals; toddlers are the blue-sky thinkers. Adults are good at executing plans, meeting deadlines and reacting fast with action plans. But children beat adults hands-down at change, imagination and learning. As Gopnik says, 'Caterpillars and butterflies do different things well'.

You're the lab assistant

In life, we need a mixture of childish imaginative speculation and mature discipline. The balance changes as we grow. If toddlers are given too much structure or planned thinking, it inhibits their intellectual development, rather than promoting it. Toddlers cannot focus for long, so expecting them to pay attention to one idea for a long time is like demanding that a butterfly flies straight. Adult brains are assisted by inhibiting chemicals that help us focus, but toddlers don't have these chemicals in the same levels (this is why they need proportionally more medication when being given a general anaesthetic). Toddlers are not being difficult – it's genuinely harder to shut down their brains!

Once you understand this about your toddler's brain, you'll find yourself behaving differently towards him. You may even find your own thinking opened up by his free-roaming exploration of the world and his delight in finding things out. You'll begin to see your role, in part, as his lab assistant, laying on all the equipment he needs, catering for his physical wellbeing, providing feedback and making sure everything is safe while your little Einstein carries on his great work of discovery.

Reason and reassurance

Your budding scientist needs emotional support too, and it's easy to underestimate the importance of this. You may think that when he gets frightened by the shadow on the bedroom wall, it's because he doesn't know what it is. So you might concentrate on getting him to understand that it's just a silly shadow. In fact, he may well know it's a shadow, but he just can't control his powerful imagination, which tells him that shadows can grow into an all-eating cloud monster. A toddler's imagination is much more vivid than an adult's. What matters in a situation like this is less a reasoned explanation than comforting cuddles and calmness, because these will help him get his own raging fears under control.

Research indicates that one key predictor of academic achievement is not a high IQ or a genius-rating store of knowledge, but the ability to control emotions. In other words, if you want a super-bright baby, the best thing you can do for him is provide the comfort, stability and guidance he needs to control his emotions. You are not trying to rein in the exploratory spirit that makes a toddler such a unique scientist and creator. You just need to be there to hug him when it gets out of hand.

Condensed idea
Toddlers are freewheeling creative scientists who need your support, not your instructions

46 Toddler books

Children don't start reading until the age of around five or six, but time spent reading to a toddler really builds on the groundwork you laid down by reading to her as a baby. Research shows that reading to toddlers is one of the most useful of all activities.

Ready to read?

Children don't form the neural connections necessary to decode letters and start putting them together until around the age of about five, so it's probably best to lay aside any letter 'flashcards' for a few years yet. However, you can continue to encourage a love of reading by spending some time every day looking at various types of books with your toddler. This can be a wonderful time, as you both travel into the world of imagination together or simply enjoy that very special kind of communication and a sense of closeness. You may have read to your toddler in her first year, when she was a baby who could not understand anything but simply appreciated being cuddled up and doing something with you. But now she's a toddler and can both understand what you read and actively engage in the story, it's a very different process that engages her brain in an entirely new way.

Reading and sharing books has obvious benefits for literacy and language skills, as well as social, emotional and cognitive development. In fact, research suggests that continuing to read to children as they grow is so valuable that it can overcome even inbuilt disadvantages such as lack of parental income. More than anything, stories are a wonderful imaginative experience, and experts are now beginning to understand that imagination is the key to a young child's mental progress.

Toddlers learn and develop brain connections through the fantastic journeys they allow their young minds to embark upon when hearing stories. They begin to learn about other lives, develop better problem-solving skills and widen their sense of possibilities. 'What if…?' becomes an adventure, and this is a great approach to develop towards life's challenges.

The old story

Most toddlers would actually be quite happy to hear you reading the annals of the Scientific Society if you read them in a lively way. They just love the interaction, however it comes. But it's much better to choose a story that will appeal to them – and you, because your toddler will soon know if you're even a tiny bit bored. Any activity that you like, she's likely to be fond of too. Conversely, anything you do unwillingly is likely to be a no-no for her, both now and in the future. So if you want to raise a child that loves books, choose books you both enjoy reading.

Ideally, aim to read to your toddler for 20 minutes or more every day. However, if she doesn't enjoy being read to, don't force her. Just try it every now and then, and you may suddenly find she changes her mind. Toddlers love the familiar, so don't be surprised if the story your toddler most wants to hear is the story she heard last night and the night before that. This repetition is actually a good thing. As your toddler learns the story, the familiarity acts to reinforce memory paths, and soon she will be able to predict what's coming. This is good for her developing brain. After a while she will know her favourite stories by heart; so well that she might appear to be reading them with you as you go through the pages.

However, it's good to add new stories to the familiar, so aim for a balance of old and new. The best way to introduce new books is to follow up on your toddler's own interests. If she likes pirates, try a new story about ships or 'baddies'. If she likes a story about bears, try one about lions. Fictional stories have a special place because they tap into a toddler's freewheeling imagination, so they're always at the heart of story time. But do try non-fiction books too. They, too, can fire the imagination and help build a store of knowledge about the world. Make your reading together interactive: show her the pictures and point out to her where you are in the story. Ask her questions about it, and encourage her to interrupt you with questions. Look out for cut-out and pop-up books too,

Rhyme time

Toddlers love rhyme because of the familiarity and the pleasure of connecting sounds. At a young age, children can recognize that 'cat' sounds like 'mat'. As they get to hear rhymes, they are also learning the phonetic constituents of words, and this is a great help in later progress to reading as they realize that words with the same sound may be spelled similarly too. Research shows that children sensitive to rhyme are noticeably quicker at learning to read, and this holds true despite any differences in income and class background.

where even the books themselves are interactive. From six months to one year old, children enjoy simple board books with interactive features. From one to two years old, they love repetitive and rhyming books, so make sure your reading includes lots of these.

Learning to read

In time, many toddlers will want to 'read' books for themselves, and it's great to make your toddler's books easy to reach, so she can flick through them whenever she wants. With familiar stories, she may know them so well that she will say the words as well as look at the pictures. It will be a while before she actually starts to read, but when you're reading with her, show her where you are on the page so

> Alicia just understood that the word on the page is the same thing I'm saying *and* it's a thing in the world. Yay! #cuddlingup

she can begin to link parts of the story with written words. Stop to sound out simple words where there's a suitable picture to help. If you've been using baby signs (see pages 100–104), you can point to a picture in a book, then show the sign for the word.

Experts disagree on the best way to promote reading. Some believe that the best way is for children to learn by practice, others argue in favour of a 'phonic' approach (breaking words into sounds). One great way to start is by putting up an alphabet frieze on a toddler's wall, so she can see how the different sounds are shown. Alphabet books also help toddlers learn how to isolate letters. As always, be guided by your child's interests.

Condensed idea
Reading regularly to a toddler stimulates imagination and curiosity

Although children cannot count properly until they are at least four years old, you can still give even the youngest toddler a helping hand by introducing him gently to the concept of numbers, sizes and quantities in the course of everyday activities such as getting dressed.

Number one

Many toddlers can recite the numbers 1–10 before they are two years old, and it's easy to be lured into thinking that they are on the road to counting. However, very few of those toddlers will have a clue what those numbers mean, however clearly they say them. Ask a toddler who 'counts' fluently to give you three buttons or five buttons and the chances are he'll just pick up the same handful!

That doesn't mean it's a waste of time trying to introduce numbers and quantities to toddlers. A 2010 study by US psychologist Susan Levine and her team at the University of Chicago was very revealing. The team monitored a group of 44 toddlers (aged 14–30 months) and their parents over several 90-minute sessions. What they discovered was a huge disparity in the number of times the parents mentioned number words in that time: from just four to over 250. While few, if any, of the toddlers had any real understanding what the numbers meant

> John counted out all the five frogs in a row in his book today. He's only two, so gave himself a round of applause. #frogprincess

at the time, when they were retested at 46 months old, those children who had been given the greatest exposure to number words had a much better understanding of what they meant than those who had been given less exposure. Levine is keen to stress that this doesn't imply a causal relationship. As she says, it may simply be, for instance, that the parents who talked most about numbers to their children did so because their children were already interested in numbers. But it may suggest that talking to toddlers about numbers and quantities from an early age could be valuable.

One for you

There are many little ways you can introduce numbers into a toddler's life without it seeming to be a chore (to your toddler or you). By far the best way is to bring numbers lightly into everyday activities so that they become part of your toddler's daily life. When you're laying the settings for tea, for instance, you could count them out: 'One spoon for daddy, one spoon for mummy and one for you. One, two, three spoons!' After a while you can ask your toddler to do the place setting, handing out

one item for each person and saying the numbers with you. Don't worry that he doesn't understand what the numbers mean; simply reciting them means he's becoming familiar with the words. He may say there are 'three spoons' when you ask him, no matter how many you've laid out – but that doesn't matter. Make little number rituals of putting on his shoes, too: 'On goes shoe number one! On goes shoe number two!'. You can do the same when you're helping him put his arms into his pullover sleeves or washing his fingers and toes. When you're counting quantities for recipes or the coins in your purse, count out loud, slowly, and let him see what you're doing. You can do the same when you're playing with him, counting out wooden blocks or animals, and getting him to do the same as he builds a tower or puts the toys away. Number rhymes and songs are a great way to introduce numbers, especially if they include actions, such as the old favourite, 'One Two, Buckle my Shoe'.

Figure hugging

When you feel the time is right, you can also start introducing your toddler to figures or numerals (1, 2, 3 and so on). You could mark the numerals 1 and 2 on his shoes and say the numbers out loud as you put the shoes on. Another way to increase daily exposure is to display the numbers 1 to 5 on the nursery wall, next to equivalent groups of little frogs, for instance. In this way numerals will become a part of his world. If you have a tablet computer, you might consider using toddler maths apps, which are very interactive. These ask the toddler to touch the screen to count cows, sheep or strawberries, for example, while the app counts along with the toddler, showing the number and 'saying' it out loud. Some apps even applaud the user each time he finishes a set of numerals.

Comparing and relativity

Familiarity with numbers does not necessarily involve understanding what numbers mean, and this is not something you need to worry about too much with a younger toddler. Nonetheless, you might be surprised to find that he will be interested in hearing about how things can be

Block learning

Blocks and boxes seem so simple that it's easy to underestimate their value in a toddler's learning. They help with motor skills, of course, as a toddler picks them up to stack them or place them inside each other. But they're also valuable for teaching him about size and quantity. When a toddler experiments with nesting boxes, he learns that big boxes won't fit inside little boxes. He learns that if he wants to build a tall tower, he must start with big bricks and then use smaller bricks, and use more bricks on the bottom than on the top. Bricks make good counters, too, if you help him.

compared, and that some things are bigger than others. For instance, if you show him that daddy's shoes are bigger than mummy's shoes and mummy's shoes are bigger than his, you'll be giving him plenty of food for thought. Encourage him to play 'Who's the biggest?' games with toy animals. Look around his world (things near his cot, in your kitchen or in the garden) for big things and small things, short things and long things. Let him help you measure large or small quantities of rice or pour different amounts of water into mugs. Ask him to help with the laundry, sorting things into piles of 'big' and 'small' clothes. Then watch – within a short time, he'll be coming up with numeric games of his own.

Condensed idea
Use everyday items to introduce the idea of number and quantity into your toddler's life

Every child is different. This sounds obvious, but it is often forgotten, even by parents and carers, who – with the best will in the world – may try to impose a caring regime that doesn't fit their own child. Toddlers respond best when you adapt your way of caring to suit them.

Siblings and difference

By the age of 18 months, it's clear that there are huge differences between children. Some are calm and relaxed. Others are feisty live wires, always on the go. Some are outgoing and bubbly; some are shy and wary. The uniqueness of every child is crystal clear to anyone that spends time with them, and those differences go on becoming more marked throughout the second year. Some of these differences are

genetic – every child inherits a unique set of genes from its parents. Yet even siblings, who inherit similar genes to one another, may grow up very differently. This may be due to their differing positions within the family. Parents learn how to do the job with their first child, who for a while is their only child. Yet they often approach things differently with the second child – and, of course, the way parents treat their second child affects their first child, too.

> Mattie really loved messy painting games, but they make his little sister cry! #queenofclean

Mum may give the new baby plenty of cuddles and attention, just as she did the first child when she arrived. But the first child has no memory of that; she may feel jealous of all those cuddles that she seems to be too old for now. She may even begin to behave like a baby to regain her mum's cuddles, often irritating mum, who's got a baby to cope with and may think (mistakenly) that her toddler should be old enough to know better.

Each family member develops his or her own particular connections and special relationships. An oldest child will relate differently to each person in the family, and her sibling will forge different relationships with these people and others. Each of these relationships will affect how the child sees herself within the family, as well as how she responds to different kinds of attention. All of this can have a huge impact on the way each child develops and the choices they make in life now and as an adult.

Bespoke upbringing

It's not possible to turn a whole family's behaviour upside down to suit each child, even if you have just one, but look out for differences in the nature and responses of each child. You'll need to make subtle adjustments to your caring in order to bring out the best in each of them, to suit their unique needs and way of being. In the past, many experts have issued blanket advice for all children, assuming that what is good for the majority is good for them all. Even the scientific research quoted in this book is based on typical child profiles and statistical averages. However, it's important to acknowledge the unique nature of your child by being sensitive to her responses and behaviour rather than persisting with an activity that apparently suits most children. This seems to suggest that you're on your own, to make your own judgements, and this is true to some extent. Every idea offered to parents – even those given in this book – is simply a starting point from which you, the only real experts on your own child, can make the right call.

Temperament traits

In their landmark studies on temperaments, psychologists Thomas and Chess highlighted the following nine traits; using them can give you an insight into your toddler's temperament:

- **Activity level:** is your toddler constantly moving or more relaxed?
- **Rhythmicity:** how regular are her sleeping and eating habits?
- **Approach/withdrawal:** does your toddler find it easy or difficult to meet new people or go to new places?
- **Adaptability to change:** do changes make her scream or smile?
- **Intensity of reaction:** do unhappy events tend to result in screaming or mild disappointment?
- **Distractability:** is your toddler easy to distract from something she's doing, or not?
- **Persistence and attention span:** if a toy or game is difficult, will she persist or give up?
- **Threshold of responsiveness:** is she easily startled or not?
- **Quality of mood:** is she generally happy or unhappy?

Different types of temperament

Landmark long-term research in New York in the 1960s by psychologists Alexander Thomas and Stella Chess has led to the idea of grouping children by 'temperaments'. This provides us with some insight and guidance in looking after children of recognizably different types. Thomas and Chess looked at nine measures (see the box, opposite), and found that two-thirds of infants can be divided into three temperament types.

First, there are easy-going, flexible children, who are happy, sleep and eat well and regularly, and are adaptable, calm and not easily upset. Second, there are more 'spirited' (once called pejoratively 'difficult') children, who are active live wires, likely to be less regular in their sleeping and eating habits, and more fussy, anxious, fearful of new people and situations, intense in their reactions, and easily upset by noise and disturbance. Third, there are the cautious, 'slow to warm' children, who are less active and more suspicious of new situations, but gradually warm with repeated positive encounters.

Of the 65 per cent of children who fit into these three temperament types, 40 per cent are 'flexible and happy'; 10 per cent are 'live wires'; and 15 per cent are 'slow to warm'. If you can identify your toddler's temperament, it makes sense to work with that, rather than against it. There's no point in trying to take a sensitive live wire into situations that another toddler might find stimulating, but your toddler simply finds upsetting. Similarly, it would be wrong to expect a cautious toddler to play readily with new friends; she needs time. The key is sensitivity, flexibility and a willingness to see what might be right for her.

Condensed idea
Recognize that your child is unique and that you need to respond to her in a very individual way

(49) Abstract thinking

For babies, the world is a 'concrete' place – a place in which they only experience and understand real things brought to them directly through their senses. But between the ages of one and two, toddlers begin to develop their first inklings of abstract thought.

Concrete and abstract

Concrete thinking involves things you can know through your senses – things you can feel, see, hear, smell, taste or touch. Abstract thinking is about mental concepts and links; love, time and manners are all abstract ideas. A child can only begin to understand abstract concepts properly at the age of around five, but that doesn't mean that a toddler can't be very loving, polite and even tell the time when asked. He just can't quite understand what it means.

During a child's second year, he can learn how to behave lovingly or politely by seeing it demonstrated concretely; that is to say, by seeing it modelled by real people in the world around him. If he sees that people are pleased by cuddles, kisses, shows of affection and expressions of care, he will follow these models. When he hears you telling him to say 'please' and 'thank you', he will also notice when you say this. The concept of 'sharing' is learned in the same way. A toddler may not understand why sharing is good, but he does see that you are pleased when he offers a toy to his sister or friend, and that's good enough for now. He wants your approval, so he will do things you approve of. However, it's useful to bear in mind that at this stage a toddler won't have actually grasped the concept, so may need constant reminders to do the thing you want.

Early ideas

Your toddler will show signs of interest in abstract thought in many ways. Perhaps he is already learning to partly categorize things, such as 'shoes' and 'hats'. He'll move from understanding what you mean by his shoe and hat, towards an idea of shoes as things that can go on people's feet, and hats as things that can go on people's heads, even though they might be all sorts of colours and shapes. This sounds like a simple thing, but recognizing the boundaries that make something one particular kind of thing and not another is a big step in cognitive development. It allows toddlers to separate and begin to make connections between things in their heads.

Towards the end of his second year, a toddler may begin to understand abstract categories such as 'family', 'rooms', 'food', 'animals', 'colours', 'shapes', 'good' and 'bad', 'before' and 'after', 'big' and 'small', 'happy'

Baby statisticians

Recent research suggests that experts may have been far too quick to write off toddlers' capacity for abstract thought. Psychologist Alison Gopnik has been at the forefront of studies which have shown that toddlers have a good intuitive grasp of probabilities; they react with surprise when a statistically improbable thing happens, such as pulling a red ball from a box of predominantly white balls. Babies also have a sophisticated understanding of cause and effect. This suggests that they are far more cognitively advanced than one might guess from their as yet scanty language skills and underdeveloped motor skills.

and 'sad'. Books can be very helpful for reinforcing the understanding of these categories. As you look together at books showing pictures of planes, boats and trains, he will begin to see that these different objects have something in common – they are all machines that carry people. Before long, he'll be able to understand the abstract idea of a plane journey, even if he's never been on a plane.

Colours and shapes are also a great way to introduce a toddler to categories. Give him toys in simple, unambiguous colours, so you can name them. Play games to see if he can find a green car, or two green cars, or all the green cars. Bring colours into your everyday talk: 'Look at the red bus', 'You're wearing your yellow shirt', and so on. See if he can help you sort the laundry into 'whites' and 'colours'. You can do the same kind of thing with shapes.

Sorting games help in the same way, so encourage him to help put away his toys in the right box, put his socks in the sock drawer, place the right cutlery in the right places and so on. There are lots of commercial sorting games and puzzles for toddlers, too, but these are essentially doing the same thing as your everyday tasks. When he's old enough, you can introduce simple stacking toys and shape sorters, then move on to more elaborate constructions made with small bricks or Lego®.

Pretend play

Perhaps the most important way in which abstract thought develops is through pretend play. A huge body of research supports the connection between intellectual development and imaginative play, showing that it can contribute to a toddler's later ability in everything from mathematics to problem solving and academic achievement. This intuitively makes sense. Just as a toddler tries things out in the physical world through sensory experiments, so

> Arjun just spent an hour filling floating eggshells with piles of sand. And laughing! #workingitout

he will experiment with mental ideas while he's playing games of make-believe. When he's imagining how this bowl could be a boat on the sea, he's experimenting with abstract ideas about boats and the sea – and what might happen there – as well as identifying connections between the shapes of boats and the shapes of bowls.

If you see your toddler enjoying games of make-believe, give him all the encouragement and help you can, in terms of props and occasional prompts. There's no need to worry about him getting lost in a fantasy world; he'll always come down to earth once he's finished playing. The more he feeds his imagination, the more his abstract thought will develop. So plant little seed thoughts to help him begin, such as: 'Teddy's sitting very upright today. Do you think he's getting ready for a big adventure?'. If possible, make time for make-believe play every day, so he can create a world in his own head that he can use for thinking things through much more easily than in the huge, complicated real world.

Condensed idea
Imaginative play will help your toddler develop symbolic and abstract thinking

50 The growing brain

Advances in scanning technology and other techniques in the past few decades have taught neuroscientists a huge amount about the developing brains of children, and every new discovery seems to reveal what a truly astonishing organ it is, from birth to old age.

Clever from birth

Parents don't need scanners or laboratories to see just how amazingly and fast their toddler's brain develops. They need only see the way she learns to walk, speak, and respond in ever more lively and curious ways to the world around her. Even though they know it's happened to billions of children before, it still seems nothing short of miraculous. Discoveries in neuroscience are beginning to show us what's actually happening. Even though a newborn's head is quite large and neurons have been growing apace throughout pregnancy, her brain still only a quarter of the size of an adult's. But over the first two years of life, more and more brain crams itself into a toddler's head, as it grows rapidly more heavy and dense. By the time she's two, her brain will be three-quarters of the size of an adult's. It's constantly abuzz with learning activity, and demands twice as much glucose energy as an adult's, too, just to keep this learning process going. Learning stimulates the development of connection after connection sprouting like the branches of a tree on superfertilizer.

> Sometimes I sit and marvel at the amazing things going on in Betty's brain – then she pretends to be a duck! #gottaloveher

This brain super-growth is not down to new nerve cells. Although new cells are continuously added after birth, this addition is quite slow. What really multiplies are the connections between cells, as their branches (known as dendrites and axons) reach out when they are stimulated by inputs, to make ever more contacts with other nerve cells. By the time your toddler is three years old, each one of the trillions of nerve cells in her brain will have made 10,000 connections, creating a total of around a quadrillion connections. Nerve cells also become much quicker at processing information, as key cells develop a sheath of myelin that not only protects them but speeds up the signal. The speed of processing accelerates dramatically during infancy and childhood, so that by the time your child is 15, her brain will be transmitting signals 16 times faster than when she was born.

A streamlined brain

However, brain development isn't all about gaining more connections and nerve cells. As a child grows older, she actually loses half her brain cells and an even bigger number of connections. During the toddler learning years, some nerves and patterns of nerve connections, known as neural networks, grow ever stronger and faster, while those that aren't stimulated wither away to concentrate brainpower where it's needed, in a process neuroscientists aptly call 'pruning'.

In the first three years of life, growth far exceeds pruning, but after that they are in balance until the age of around 10. At this stage pruning begins to dominate, as thought processing becomes more streamlined and efficient. A child's brain is continuously shaped by this play-off between growth and pruning. Learning is about stimulating the right networks and allowing those unstimulated to be pruned away. Even during adult life, the interplay between growth and loss is ever-changing. When parts of the body are frequently used, for instance,

Sensations in the brain

Whenever a toddler experiences a new sensation, it starts a cascade of events in her developing brain. First, a flurry of activity surges through particular tangles of neurons. Each neuron involved then passes on its message to other neurons, while also sending a signal back to the neurons that alerted it, creating a feedback loop. This amplifies the signal or damps it down.

After the initial stimulus passes, the neurons involved reinforce their connections with one another – they have formed an association. Now they are primed and ready to fire again easily if the same sensation comes in, like a well-trodden path through the brain. Mum's footsteps in the hall are linked to being lifted and kissed, for instance. If the sensation is not repeated (a dog barks and the baby is kissed, for instance) the connections fade.

the area of the brain devoted to them grows. Scans of the brains of violin players show that the area of the brain devoted to the thumb and fourth finger of the left hand (used to grip the violin neck and finger the strings) is much larger than normal. The younger the violinist started to play, the larger this area of the brain. This is because the more you stimulate areas of the brain with inputs, the bigger and stronger they grow. But before you force a violin into your toddler's hand in the hope of making her a future Paganini, remember that growth in one area may inhibit growth in another.

Prime time

Neuroscientists have begun to realize there may be critical periods in a young life when particular networks are best stimulated. The theory is that a young brain is specially primed within certain narrow windows to respond to important stimuli that activate particular networks. If those stimuli are weak or missed at this time, the networks don't develop as much. When a baby is born, for instance, she can clearly distinguish the unique sounds of all the languages of the world. But unless she hears these sounds, this remarkable ability is lost: only the aural brain pathways for the sounds of the language she hears are kept; the rest are discarded.

In all of this science, one thing is clear – the only one thing that really matters in every baby's life is loving care and attention. The bond between carer and child is at the heart of not just every emotional development but intellectual development too, in a very real and physical way. A baby who is loved and encouraged to discover the world for herself has every chance of growing to be a super-bright child in the best sense – a shining, loving spirit who sees life as an opportunity to fulfil her potential.

Condensed idea
The brain changes constantly, reinforcing repeated thoughts and behaviours

Index

Picture credits

Incidental images used throughout.
Fotolia: Accent; TAlex; Alfaolga; Allison; Anna; Roman Dekan; Draganm; Elinor33; Didem Hizar; HuHu Lin; Pavel Losevsky; Mayboro; Oksun70; Alexander Potapov; Tpandd;
Shutterstock: Potapov Alexander; W. Jarva
iStockphoto: Bubaone

Quercus Publishing Plc
55 Baker Street, 7th Floor,
South Block, London W1U 8EW

First published in 2013

A catalogue record of this book is available from the British Library

ISBN 978 1 78206 136 6

Printed and bound in China

10 9 8 7 6 5 4 3 2 1

Produced for Quercus Publishing Plc by
Tracy Killick Art Direction and Design

Commissioning editor: Sarah Tomley
(of www.editorsonline.org)
Designer: Tracy Killick
Project editor: Alice Bowden
Proof-reader: Louise Abbott
Illustrator: Victoria Woodgate
(www.vickywoodgate.com)
Indexer: Hilary Bird